MW00948514

This Book Belongs To

KEEP A GOOD THING GOING

EVERYDAY

	S	M	T	W	T	F	S
ONE LOAD OF LAUNDRY	◆	◆	◆	◆	◆	◆	◆
DISHES	◆	◆	◆	◆	◆	◆	◆
MAKE BEDS	◆	◆	◆	◆	◆	◆	◆
SPARY COUNTERTOPS	◆	◆	◆	◆	◆	◆	◆
PICK UP CLUTTER	◆	◆	◆	◆	◆	◆	◆
TRASH	◆	◆	◆	◆	◆	◆	◆
SORT MAIL	◆	◆	◆	◆	◆	◆	◆

MONTHLY

- DUST CEILING FANS
- CLEAN OVEN
- CLEAN INSIDE OF FRIDGE
- WASH WINDOWS
- PICK UP GARAGE
- PICK UP BASEMENT
- DUST/CLEAN BASEBOARDS
- GET RID OF ITEMS NO LONGER NEED
- ------------------------------
- ------------------------------
- ------------------------------
-

MON — KITCHEN
- ★ CLEAN KITCHEN TABLE
- ★ WIPE DOWN SINK AND COUNTERS
- ★ VACUUM OR MOP
- ★ WIPE DOWN APPLIANCES
- ★

TUES — LIVINGROOM
- ★ PICK UP CLUTTER
- ★ VACUUM OR MOP
- ★ WASH BLANKETS
- ★ DUST SURFACES
- ★

WED — BEDROOM
- ★ PUT AWAY CLOTHES/PICK UP CLUTTER
- ★ DUST SURFACES
- ★ WASH BEDDING
- ★ VACUUM OR MOP
- ★

THUR — BATHROOM
- ★ SANITIZE TOILET
- ★ VACUUM OR MOP
- ★ WASH SHOWER,SINK AND MIRRORS
- ★ WASH TOWELS AND MATS
- ★

FRI — DINING
- ★ CLEAN OFF TABLE
- ★ VACUUM OR MOP
- ★ DUST SURFACES
- ★ PICK UP CLUTTER
- ★

SAT — ENTRY
- ★ SANTIZE DOORKNOBS
- ★ DUST SURFACES
- ★ VACUUM OR MOP
- ★ PUT AWAY SHOES/COATS/HATS
- ★

SUN — GROCERY
- ★ CLEAN OUT FRIDGE
- ★ MEAL PLAN
- ★ GROCERY SHOP AND FILL GAS TANK
- ★ MEAL PREP
- ★

DATE :

CLEANING CHEEKLIST

KEEP A GOOD THING GOING

EVERYDAY

	S	M	T	W	T	F	S
ONE LOAD OF LAUNDRY	◆	◆	◆	◆	◆	◆	◆
DISHES	◆	◆	◆	◆	◆	◆	◆
MAKE BEDS	◆	◆	◆	◆	◆	◆	◆
SPARY COUNTERTOPS	◆	◆	◆	◆	◆	◆	◆
PICK UP CLUTTER	◆	◆	◆	◆	◆	◆	◆
TRASH	◆	◆	◆	◆	◆	◆	◆
SORT MAIL	◆	◆	◆	◆	◆	◆	◆

MONTHLY

- DUST CEILING FANS
- CLEAN OVEN
- CLEAN INSIDE OF FRIDGE
- WASH WINDOWS
- PICK UP GARAGE
- PICK UP BASEMENT
- DUST/CLEAN BASEBOARDS
- GET RID OF ITEMS NO LONGER NEED
- _____
- _____
- _____
- _____

MON — KITCHEN
- ★ CLEAN KITCHEN TABLE
- ★ WIPE DOWN SINK AND COUNTERS
- ★ VACUUM OR MOP
- ★ WIPE DOWN APPLIANCES
- ★

TUES — LIVING ROOM
- ★ PICK UP CLUTTER
- ★ VACUUM OR MOP
- ★ WASH BLANKETS
- ★ DUST SURFACES
- ★

WED — BEDROOM
- ★ PUT AWAY CLOTHES/PICK UP CLUTTER
- ★ DUST SURFACES
- ★ WASH BEDDING
- ★ VACUUM OR MOP
- ★

THUR — BATHROOM
- ★ SANITIZE TOILET
- ★ VACUUM OR MOP
- ★ WASH SHOWER,SINK AND MIRRORS
- ★ WASH TOWELS AND MATS
- ★

FRI — DINING
- ★ CLEAN OFF TABLE
- ★ VACUUM OR MOP
- ★ DUST SURFACES
- ★ PICK UP CLUTTER
- ★

SAT — ENTRY
- ★ SANTIZE DOORKNOBS
- ★ DUST SURFACES
- ★ VACUUM OR MOP
- ★ PUT AWAY SHOES/COATS/HATS
- ★

SUN — GROCERY
- ★ CLEAN OUT FRIDGE
- ★ MEAL PLAN
- ★ GROCERY SHOP AND FILL GAS TANK
- ★ MEAL PREP
- ★

DATE :

CLEANING CHEEKLIST

KEEP A GOOD THING GOING

EVERYDAY

	S	M	T	W	T	F	S
ONE LOAD OF LAUNDRY	◆	◆	◆	◆	◆	◆	◆
DISHES	◆	◆	◆	◆	◆	◆	◆
MAKE BEDS	◆	◆	◆	◆	◆	◆	◆
SPARY COUNTERTOPS	◆	◆	◆	◆	◆	◆	◆
PICK UP CLUTTER	◆	◆	◆	◆	◆	◆	◆
TRASH	◆	◆	◆	◆	◆	◆	◆
SORT MAIL	◆	◆	◆	◆	◆	◆	◆

MONTHLY

- DUST CEILING FANS
- CLEAN OVEN
- CLEAN INSIDE OF FRIDGE
- WASH WINDOWS
- PICK UP GARAGE
- PICK UP BASEMENT
- DUST/CLEAN BASEBOARDS
- GET RID OF ITEMS NO LONGER NEED
- -------------------------------
- -------------------------------
- -------------------------------
-

MON	KITCHEN	★ CLEAN KITCHEN TABLE ★ WIPE DOWN SINK AND COUNTERS ★ VACUUM OR MOP ★ WIPE DOWN APPLIANCES ★
TUES	LIVING ROOM	★ PICK UP CLUTTER ★ VACUUM OR MOP ★ WASH BLANKETS ★ DUST SURFACES ★
WED	BEDROOM	★ PUT AWAY CLOTHES/PICK UP CLUTTER ★ DUST SURFACES ★ WASH BEDDING ★ VACUUM OR MOP ★
THUR	BATHROOM	★ SANITIZE TOILET ★ VACUUM OR MOP ★ WASH SHOWER,SINK AND MIRRORS ★ WASH TOWELS AND MATS ★
FRI	DINING	★ CLEAN OFF TABLE ★ VACUUM OR MOP ★ DUST SURFACES ★ PICK UP CLUTTER ★
SAT	ENTRY	★ SANTIZE DOORKNOBS ★ DUST SURFACES ★ VACUUM OR MOP ★ PUT AWAY SHOES/COATS/HATS ★
SUN	GROCERY	★ CLEAN OUT FRIDGE ★ MEAL PLAN ★ GROCERY SHOP AND FILL GAS TANK ★ MEAL PREP ★

DATE:

CLEANING CHEEKLIST

KEEP A GOOD THING GOING

EVERYDAY

	S	M	T	W	T	F	S
ONE LOAD OF LAUNDRY	◆	◆	◆	◆	◆	◆	◆
DISHES	◆	◆	◆	◆	◆	◆	◆
MAKE BEDS	◆	◆	◆	◆	◆	◆	◆
SPARY COUNTERTOPS	◆	◆	◆	◆	◆	◆	◆
PICK UP CLUTTER	◆	◆	◆	◆	◆	◆	◆
TRASH	◆	◆	◆	◆	◆	◆	◆
SORT MAIL	◆	◆	◆	◆	◆	◆	◆

MONTHLY

- DUST CEILING FANS
- CLEAN OVEN
- CLEAN INSIDE OF FRIDGE
- WASH WINDOWS
- PICK UP GARAGE
- PICK UP BASEMENT
- DUST/CLEAN BASEBOARDS
- GET RID OF ITEMS NO LONGER NEED
- _____
- _____
- _____
- _____

MON	KITCHEN	★ CLEAN KITCHEN TABLE ★ WIPE DOWN SINK AND COUNTERS ★ VACUUM OR MOP ★ WIPE DOWN APPLIANCES ★
TUES	LIVING ROOM	★ PICK UP CLUTTER ★ VACUUM OR MOP ★ WASH BLANKETS ★ DUST SURFACES ★
WED	BEDROOM	★ PUT AWAY CLOTHES/PICK UP CLUTTER ★ DUST SURFACES ★ WASH BEDDING ★ VACUUM OR MOP ★
THUR	BATHROOM	★ SANITIZE TOILET ★ VACUUM OR MOP ★ WASH SHOWER, SINK AND MIRRORS ★ WASH TOWELS AND MATS ★
FRI	DINING	★ CLEAN OFF TABLE ★ VACUUM OR MOP ★ DUST SURFACES ★ PICK UP CLUTTER ★
SAT	ENTRY	★ SANTIZE DOORKNOBS ★ DUST SURFACES ★ VACUUM OR MOP ★ PUT AWAY SHOES/COATS/HATS ★
SUN	GROCERY	★ CLEAN OUT FRIDGE ★ MEAL PLAN ★ GROCERY SHOP AND FILL GAS TANK ★ MEAL PREP ★

CLEANING CHEEKLIST

KEEP A GOOD THING GOING

EVERYDAY

	S	M	T	W	T	F	S
ONE LOAD OF LAUNDRY	◆	◆	◆	◆	◆	◆	◆
DISHES	◆	◆	◆	◆	◆	◆	◆
MAKE BEDS	◆	◆	◆	◆	◆	◆	◆
SPARY COUNTERTOPS	◆	◆	◆	◆	◆	◆	◆
PICK UP CLUTTER	◆	◆	◆	◆	◆	◆	◆
TRASH	◆	◆	◆	◆	◆	◆	◆
SORT MAIL	◆	◆	◆	◆	◆	◆	◆

MONTHLY

- DUST CEILING FANS
- CLEAN OVEN
- CLEAN INSIDE OF FRIDGE
- WASH WINDOWS
- PICK UP GARAGE
- PICK UP BASEMENT
- DUST/CLEAN BASEBOARDS
- GET RID OF ITEMS NO LONGER NEED
- ------------------------------
- ------------------------------
- ------------------------------
- ------------------------------

MON	KITCHEN	☆ CLEAN KITCHEN TABLE ☆ WIPE DOWN SINK AND COUNTERS ☆ VACUUM OR MOP ☆ WIPE DOWN APPLIANCES ☆
TUES	LIVINGROOM	☆ PICK UP CLUTTER ☆ VACUUM OR MOP ☆ WASH BLANKETS ☆ DUST SURFACES ☆
WED	BEDROOM	☆ PUT AWAY CLOTHES/PICK UP CLUTTER ☆ DUST SURFACES ☆ WASH BEDDING ☆ VACUUM OR MOP ☆
THUR	BATHROOM	☆ SANITIZE TOILET ☆ VACUUM OR MOP ☆ WASH SHOWER,SINK AND MIRRORS ☆ WASH TOWELS AND MATS ☆
FRI	DINING	☆ CLEAN OFF TABLE ☆ VACUUM OR MOP ☆ DUST SURFACES ☆ PICK UP CLUTTER ☆
SAT	ENTRY	☆ SANTIZE DOORKNOBS ☆ DUST SURFACES ☆ VACUUM OR MOP ☆ PUT AWAY SHOES/COATS/HATS ☆
SUN	GROCERY	☆ CLEAN OUT FRIDGE ☆ MEAL PLAN ☆ GROCERY SHOP AND FILL GAS TANK ☆ MEAL PREP ☆

DATE :

CLEANING CHEEKLIST

KEEP A GOOD THING GOING

EVERYDAY

	S	M	T	W	T	F	S
ONE LOAD OF LAUNDRY	◆	◆	◆	◆	◆	◆	◆
DISHES	◆	◆	◆	◆	◆	◆	◆
MAKE BEDS	◆	◆	◆	◆	◆	◆	◆
SPARY COUNTERTOPS	◆	◆	◆	◆	◆	◆	◆
PICK UP CLUTTER	◆	◆	◆	◆	◆	◆	◆
TRASH	◆	◆	◆	◆	◆	◆	◆
SORT MAIL	◆	◆	◆	◆	◆	◆	◆

MONTHLY

- ⬡ DUST CEILING FANS
- ⬡ CLEAN OVEN
- ⬡ CLEAN INSIDE OF FRIDGE
- ⬡ WASH WINDOWS
- ⬡ PICK UP GARAGE
- ⬡ PICK UP BASEMENT
- ⬡ DUST/CLEAN BASEBOARDS
- ⬡ GET RID OF ITEMS NO LONGER NEED
- ⬡ -------------------------------
- ⬡ -------------------------------
- ⬡ -------------------------------
- ⬡ -------------------------------

MON — KITCHEN
- ★ CLEAN KITCHEN TABLE
- ★ WIPE DOWN SINK AND COUNTERS
- ★ VACUUM OR MOP
- ★ WIPE DOWN APPLIANCES
- ★

TUES — LIVINGROOM
- ★ PICK UP CLUTTER
- ★ VACUUM OR MOP
- ★ WASH BLANKETS
- ★ DUST SURFACES
- ★

WED — BEDROOM
- ★ PUT AWAY CLOTHES/PICK UP CLUTTER
- ★ DUST SURFACES
- ★ WASH BEDDING
- ★ VACUUM OR MOP
- ★

THUR — BATHROOM
- ★ SANITIZE TOILET
- ★ VACUUM OR MOP
- ★ WASH SHOWER, SINK AND MIRRORS
- ★ WASH TOWELS AND MATS
- ★

FRI — DINING
- ★ CLEAN OFF TABLE
- ★ VACUUM OR MOP
- ★ DUST SURFACES
- ★ PICK UP CLUTTER
- ★

SAT — ENTRY
- ★ SANTIZE DOORKNOBS
- ★ DUST SURFACES
- ★ VACUUM OR MOP
- ★ PUT AWAY SHOES/COATS/HATS
- ★

SUN — GROCERY
- ★ CLEAN OUT FRIDGE
- ★ MEAL PLAN
- ★ GROCERY SHOP AND FILL GAS TANK
- ★ MEAL PREP
- ★

DATE :

CLEANING CHEEKLIST

KEEP A GOOD THING GOING

EVERYDAY

	S	M	T	W	T	F	S
ONE LOAD OF LAUNDRY	◆	◆	◆	◆	◆	◆	◆
DISHES	◆	◆	◆	◆	◆	◆	◆
MAKE BEDS	◆	◆	◆	◆	◆	◆	◆
SPARY COUNTERTOPS	◆	◆	◆	◆	◆	◆	◆
PICK UP CLUTTER	◆	◆	◆	◆	◆	◆	◆
TRASH	◆	◆	◆	◆	◆	◆	◆
SORT MAIL	◆	◆	◆	◆	◆	◆	◆

MONTHLY

- ⬡ DUST CEILING FANS
- ⬡ CLEAN OVEN
- ⬡ CLEAN INSIDE OF FRIDGE
- ⬡ WASH WINDOWS
- ⬡ PICK UP GARAGE
- ⬡ PICK UP BASEMENT
- ⬡ DUST/CLEAN BASEBOARDS
- ⬡ GET RID OF ITEMS NO LONGER NEED
- ⬡ -
- ⬡ -
- ⬡ -
- ⬡ -

MON — KITCHEN
- ★ CLEAN KITCHEN TABLE
- ★ WIPE DOWN SINK AND COUNTERS
- ★ VACUUM OR MOP
- ★ WIPE DOWN APPLIANCES
- ★

TUES — LIVINGROOM
- ★ PICK UP CLUTTER
- ★ VACUUM OR MOP
- ★ WASH BLANKETS
- ★ DUST SURFACES
- ★

WED — BEDROOM
- ★ PUT AWAY CLOTHES/PICK UP CLUTTER
- ★ DUST SURFACES
- ★ WASH BEDDING
- ★ VACUUM OR MOP
- ★

THUR — BATHROOM
- ★ SANITIZE TOILET
- ★ VACUUM OR MOP
- ★ WASH SHOWER,SINK AND MIRRORS
- ★ WASH TOWELS AND MATS
- ★

FRI — DINING
- ★ CLEAN OFF TABLE
- ★ VACUUM OR MOP
- ★ DUST SURFACES
- ★ PICK UP CLUTTER
- ★

SAT — ENTRY
- ★ SANTIZE DOORKNOBS
- ★ DUST SURFACES
- ★ VACUUM OR MOP
- ★ PUT AWAY SHOES/COATS/HATS
- ★

SUN — GROCERY
- ★ CLEAN OUT FRIDGE
- ★ MEAL PLAN
- ★ GROCERY SHOP AND FILL GAS TANK
- ★ MEAL PREP
- ★

DATE :

CLEANING CHEEKLIST

KEEP A GOOD THING GOING

EVERYDAY

	S	M	T	W	T	F	S
ONE LOAD OF LAUNDRY	◆	◆	◆	◆	◆	◆	◆
DISHES	◆	◆	◆	◆	◆	◆	◆
MAKE BEDS	◆	◆	◆	◆	◆	◆	◆
SPARY COUNTERTOPS	◆	◆	◆	◆	◆	◆	◆
PICK UP CLUTTER	◆	◆	◆	◆	◆	◆	◆
TRASH	◆	◆	◆	◆	◆	◆	◆
SORT MAIL	◆	◆	◆	◆	◆	◆	◆

MONTHLY

- ⬡ DUST CEILING FANS
- ⬡ CLEAN OVEN
- ⬡ CLEAN INSIDE OF FRIDGE
- ⬡ WASH WINDOWS
- ⬡ PICK UP GARAGE
- ⬡ PICK UP BASEMENT
- ⬡ DUST/CLEAN BASEBOARDS
- ⬡ GET RID OF ITEMS NO LONGER NEED
- ⬡ -
- ⬡ -
- ⬡ -
- ⬡ -

MON — KITCHEN
- ★ CLEAN KITCHEN TABLE
- ★ WIPE DOWN SINK AND COUNTERS
- ★ VACUUM OR MOP
- ★ WIPE DOWN APPLIANCES
- ★

TUES — LIVINGROOM
- ★ PICK UP CLUTTER
- ★ VACUUM OR MOP
- ★ WASH BLANKETS
- ★ DUST SURFACES
- ★

WED — BEDROOM
- ★ PUT AWAY CLOTHES/PICK UP CLUTTER
- ★ DUST SURFACES
- ★ WASH BEDDING
- ★ VACUUM OR MOP
- ★

THUR — BATHROOM
- ★ SANITIZE TOILET
- ★ VACUUM OR MOP
- ★ WASH SHOWER, SINK AND MIRRORS
- ★ WASH TOWELS AND MATS
- ★

FRI — DINING
- ★ CLEAN OFF TABLE
- ★ VACUUM OR MOP
- ★ DUST SURFACES
- ★ PICK UP CLUTTER
- ★

SAT — ENTRY
- ★ SANTIZE DOORKNOBS
- ★ DUST SURFACES
- ★ VACUUM OR MOP
- ★ PUT AWAY SHOES/COATS/HATS
- ★

SUN — GROCERY
- ★ CLEAN OUT FRIDGE
- ★ MEAL PLAN
- ★ GROCERY SHOP AND FILL GAS TANK
- ★ MEAL PREP
- ★

DATE :

CLEANING CHEEKLIST

KEEP A GOOD THING GOING

EVERYDAY

	S	M	T	W	T	F	S
ONE LOAD OF LAUNDRY	◆	◆	◆	◆	◆	◆	◆
DISHES	◆	◆	◆	◆	◆	◆	◆
MAKE BEDS	◆	◆	◆	◆	◆	◆	◆
SPARY COUNTERTOPS	◆	◆	◆	◆	◆	◆	◆
PICK UP CLUTTER	◆	◆	◆	◆	◆	◆	◆
TRASH	◆	◆	◆	◆	◆	◆	◆
SORT MAIL	◆	◆	◆	◆	◆	◆	◆

MONTHLY

- DUST CEILING FANS
- CLEAN OVEN
- CLEAN INSIDE OF FRIDGE
- WASH WINDOWS
- PICK UP GARAGE
- PICK UP BASEMENT
- DUST/CLEAN BASEBOARDS
- GET RID OF ITEMS NO LONGER NEED
- _____
- _____
- _____
- _____

MON	KITCHEN	★ CLEAN KITCHEN TABLE ★ WIPE DOWN SINK AND COUNTERS ★ VACUUM OR MOP ★ WIPE DOWN APPLIANCES ★
TUES	LIVING ROOM	★ PICK UP CLUTTER ★ VACUUM OR MOP ★ WASH BLANKETS ★ DUST SURFACES ★
WED	BEDROOM	★ PUT AWAY CLOTHES/PICK UP CLUTTER ★ DUST SURFACES ★ WASH BEDDING ★ VACUUM OR MOP ★
THUR	BATHROOM	★ SANITIZE TOILET ★ VACUUM OR MOP ★ WASH SHOWER,SINK AND MIRRORS ★ WASH TOWELS AND MATS ★
FRI	DINING	★ CLEAN OFF TABLE ★ VACUUM OR MOP ★ DUST SURFACES ★ PICK UP CLUTTER ★
SAT	ENTRY	★ SANTIZE DOORKNOBS ★ DUST SURFACES ★ VACUUM OR MOP ★ PUT AWAY SHOES/COATS/HATS ★
SUN	GROCERY	★ CLEAN OUT FRIDGE ★ MEAL PLAN ★ GROCERY SHOP AND FILL GAS TANK ★ MEAL PREP ★

DATE :

CLEANING CHEEKLIST

KEEP A GOOD THING GOING

EVERYDAY

	S	M	T	W	T	F	S
ONE LOAD OF LAUNDRY	◆	◆	◆	◆	◆	◆	◆
DISHES	◆	◆	◆	◆	◆	◆	◆
MAKE BEDS	◆	◆	◆	◆	◆	◆	◆
SPARY COUNTERTOPS	◆	◆	◆	◆	◆	◆	◆
PICK UP CLUTTER	◆	◆	◆	◆	◆	◆	◆
TRASH	◆	◆	◆	◆	◆	◆	◆
SORT MAIL	◆	◆	◆	◆	◆	◆	◆

MONTHLY

- DUST CEILING FANS
- CLEAN OVEN
- CLEAN INSIDE OF FRIDGE
- WASH WINDOWS
- PICK UP GARAGE
- PICK UP BASEMENT
- DUST/CLEAN BASEBOARDS
- GET RID OF ITEMS NO LONGER NEED
- _____
- _____
- _____
-

MON	KITCHEN	☆ CLEAN KITCHEN TABLE ☆ WIPE DOWN SINK AND COUNTERS ☆ VACUUM OR MOP ☆ WIPE DOWN APPLIANCES ☆
TUES	LIVINGROOM	☆ PICK UP CLUTTER ☆ VACUUM OR MOP ☆ WASH BLANKETS ☆ DUST SURFACES ☆
WED	BEDROOM	☆ PUT AWAY CLOTHES/PICK UP CLUTTER ☆ DUST SURFACES ☆ WASH BEDDING ☆ VACUUM OR MOP ☆
THUR	BATHROOM	☆ SANITIZE TOILET ☆ VACUUM OR MOP ☆ WASH SHOWER,SINK AND MIRRORS ☆ WASH TOWELS AND MATS ☆
FRI	DINING	☆ CLEAN OFF TABLE ☆ VACUUM OR MOP ☆ DUST SURFACES ☆ PICK UP CLUTTER ☆
SAT	ENTRY	☆ SANTIZE DOORKNOBS ☆ DUST SURFACES ☆ VACUUM OR MOP ☆ PUT AWAY SHOES/COATS/HATS ☆
SUN	GROCERY	☆ CLEAN OUT FRIDGE ☆ MEAL PLAN ☆ GROCERY SHOP AND FILL GAS TANK ☆ MEAL PREP ☆

CLEANING CHEEKLIST

KEEP A GOOD THING GOING

EVERYDAY

	S	M	T	W	T	F	S
ONE LOAD OF LAUNDRY	◆	◆	◆	◆	◆	◆	◆
DISHES	◆	◆	◆	◆	◆	◆	◆
MAKE BEDS	◆	◆	◆	◆	◆	◆	◆
SPARY COUNTERTOPS	◆	◆	◆	◆	◆	◆	◆
PICK UP CLUTTER	◆	◆	◆	◆	◆	◆	◆
TRASH	◆	◆	◆	◆	◆	◆	◆
SORT MAIL	◆	◆	◆	◆	◆	◆	◆

MONTHLY

- DUST CEILING FANS
- CLEAN OVEN
- CLEAN INSIDE OF FRIDGE
- WASH WINDOWS
- PICK UP GARAGE
- PICK UP BASEMENT
- DUST/CLEAN BASEBOARDS
- GET RID OF ITEMS NO LONGER NEED
- _____
- _____
- _____
- _____

MON — KITCHEN
- ★ CLEAN KITCHEN TABLE
- ★ WIPE DOWN SINK AND COUNTERS
- ★ VACUUM OR MOP
- ★ WIPE DOWN APPLIANCES
- ★

TUES — LIVINGROOM
- ★ PICK UP CLUTTER
- ★ VACUUM OR MOP
- ★ WASH BLANKETS
- ★ DUST SURFACES
- ★

WED — BEDROOM
- ★ PUT AWAY CLOTHES/PICK UP CLUTTER
- ★ DUST SURFACES
- ★ WASH BEDDING
- ★ VACUUM OR MOP
- ★

THUR — BATHROOM
- ★ SANITIZE TOILET
- ★ VACUUM OR MOP
- ★ WASH SHOWER,SINK AND MIRRORS
- ★ WASH TOWELS AND MATS
- ★

FRI — DINING
- ★ CLEAN OFF TABLE
- ★ VACUUM OR MOP
- ★ DUST SURFACES
- ★ PICK UP CLUTTER
- ★

SAT — ENTRY
- ★ SANTIZE DOORKNOBS
- ★ DUST SURFACES
- ★ VACUUM OR MOP
- ★ PUT AWAY SHOES/COATS/HATS
- ★

SUN — GROCERY
- ★ CLEAN OUT FRIDGE
- ★ MEAL PLAN
- ★ GROCERY SHOP AND FILL GAS TANK
- ★ MEAL PREP
- ★

DATE :

CLEANING CHEEKLIST

KEEP A GOOD THING GOING

EVERYDAY

	S	M	T	W	T	F	S
ONE LOAD OF LAUNDRY	◆	◆	◆	◆	◆	◆	◆
DISHES	◆	◆	◆	◆	◆	◆	◆
MAKE BEDS	◆	◆	◆	◆	◆	◆	◆
SPARY COUNTERTOPS	◆	◆	◆	◆	◆	◆	◆
PICK UP CLUTTER	◆	◆	◆	◆	◆	◆	◆
TRASH	◆	◆	◆	◆	◆	◆	◆
SORT MAIL	◆	◆	◆	◆	◆	◆	◆

MONTHLY

- DUST CEILING FANS
- CLEAN OVEN
- CLEAN INSIDE OF FRIDGE
- WASH WINDOWS
- PICK UP GARAGE
- PICK UP BASEMENT
- DUST/CLEAN BASEBOARDS
- GET RID OF ITEMS NO LONGER NEED
- ------------------------------
- ------------------------------
- ------------------------------
- ------------------------------

MON	KITCHEN	☆ CLEAN KITCHEN TABLE ☆ WIPE DOWN SINK AND COUNTERS ☆ VACUUM OR MOP ☆ WIPE DOWN APPLIANCES ☆
TUES	LIVING ROOM	☆ PICK UP CLUTTER ☆ VACUUM OR MOP ☆ WASH BLANKETS ☆ DUST SURFACES ☆
WED	BEDROOM	☆ PUT AWAY CLOTHES/PICK UP CLUTTER ☆ DUST SURFACES ☆ WASH BEDDING ☆ VACUUM OR MOP ☆
THUR	BATHROOM	☆ SANITIZE TOILET ☆ VACUUM OR MOP ☆ WASH SHOWER,SINK AND MIRRORS ☆ WASH TOWELS AND MATS ☆
FRI	DINING	☆ CLEAN OFF TABLE ☆ VACUUM OR MOP ☆ DUST SURFACES ☆ PICK UP CLUTTER ☆
SAT	ENTRY	☆ SANTIZE DOORKNOBS ☆ DUST SURFACES ☆ VACUUM OR MOP ☆ PUT AWAY SHOES/COATS/HATS ☆
SUN	GROCERY	☆ CLEAN OUT FRIDGE ☆ MEAL PLAN ☆ GROCERY SHOP AND FILL GAS TANK ☆ MEAL PREP ☆

DATE :

CLEANING CHEEKLIST

KEEP A GOOD THING GOING

EVERYDAY

	S	M	T	W	T	F	S
ONE LOAD OF LAUNDRY	◈	◈	◈	◈	◈	◈	◈
DISHES	◈	◈	◈	◈	◈	◈	◈
MAKE BEDS	◈	◈	◈	◈	◈	◈	◈
SPARY COUNTERTOPS	◈	◈	◈	◈	◈	◈	◈
PICK UP CLUTTER	◈	◈	◈	◈	◈	◈	◈
TRASH	◈	◈	◈	◈	◈	◈	◈
SORT MAIL	◈	◈	◈	◈	◈	◈	◈

MONTHLY

- DUST CEILING FANS
- CLEAN OVEN
- CLEAN INSIDE OF FRIDGE
- WASH WINDOWS
- PICK UP GARAGE
- PICK UP BASEMENT
- DUST/CLEAN BASEBOARDS
- GET RID OF ITEMS NO LONGER NEED
- ----------------------------
- ----------------------------
- ----------------------------
-

MON — KITCHEN
- ★ CLEAN KITCHEN TABLE
- ★ WIPE DOWN SINK AND COUNTERS
- ★ VACUUM OR MOP
- ★ WIPE DOWN APPLIANCES
- ★

TUES — LIVING ROOM
- ★ PICK UP CLUTTER
- ★ VACUUM OR MOP
- ★ WASH BLANKETS
- ★ DUST SURFACES
- ★

WED — BEDROOM
- ★ PUT AWAY CLOTHES/PICK UP CLUTTER
- ★ DUST SURFACES
- ★ WASH BEDDING
- ★ VACUUM OR MOP
- ★

THUR — BATHROOM
- ★ SANITIZE TOILET
- ★ VACUUM OR MOP
- ★ WASH SHOWER,SINK AND MIRRORS
- ★ WASH TOWELS AND MATS
- ★

FRI — DINING
- ★ CLEAN OFF TABLE
- ★ VACUUM OR MOP
- ★ DUST SURFACES
- ★ PICK UP CLUTTER
- ★

SAT — ENTRY
- ★ SANTIZE DOORKNOBS
- ★ DUST SURFACES
- ★ VACUUM OR MOP
- ★ PUT AWAY SHOES/COATS/HATS
- ★

SUN — GROCERY
- ★ CLEAN OUT FRIDGE
- ★ MEAL PLAN
- ★ GROCERY SHOP AND FILL GAS TANK
- ★ MEAL PREP
- ★

DATE :

CLEANING CHEEKLIST

KEEP A GOOD THING GOING

EVERYDAY

	S	M	T	W	T	F	S
ONE LOAD OF LAUNDRY	◆	◆	◆	◆	◆	◆	◆
DISHES	◆	◆	◆	◆	◆	◆	◆
MAKE BEDS	◆	◆	◆	◆	◆	◆	◆
SPARY COUNTERTOPS	◆	◆	◆	◆	◆	◆	◆
PICK UP CLUTTER	◆	◆	◆	◆	◆	◆	◆
TRASH	◆	◆	◆	◆	◆	◆	◆
SORT MAIL	◆	◆	◆	◆	◆	◆	◆

MONTHLY

- ⬡ DUST CEILING FANS
- ⬡ CLEAN OVEN
- ⬡ CLEAN INSIDE OF FRIDGE
- ⬡ WASH WINDOWS
- ⬡ PICK UP GARAGE
- ⬡ PICK UP BASEMENT
- ⬡ DUST/CLEAN BASEBOARDS
- ⬡ GET RID OF ITEMS NO LONGER NEED
- ⬡ --------------------------------
- ⬡ --------------------------------
- ⬡ --------------------------------
- ⬡ --------------------------------

MON	KITCHEN	★ CLEAN KITCHEN TABLE ★ WIPE DOWN SINK AND COUNTERS ★ VACUUM OR MOP ★ WIPE DOWN APPLIANCES ★
TUES	LIVINGROOM	★ PICK UP CLUTTER ★ VACUUM OR MOP ★ WASH BLANKETS ★ DUST SURFACES ★
WED	BEDROOM	★ PUT AWAY CLOTHES/PICK UP CLUTTER ★ DUST SURFACES ★ WASH BEDDING ★ VACUUM OR MOP ★
THUR	BATHROOM	★ SANITIZE TOILET ★ VACUUM OR MOP ★ WASH SHOWER,SINK AND MIRRORS ★ WASH TOWELS AND MATS ★
FRI	DINING	★ CLEAN OFF TABLE ★ VACUUM OR MOP ★ DUST SURFACES ★ PICK UP CLUTTER ★
SAT	ENTRY	★ SANTIZE DOORKNOBS ★ DUST SURFACES ★ VACUUM OR MOP ★ PUT AWAY SHOES/COATS/HATS ★
SUN	GROCERY	★ CLEAN OUT FRIDGE ★ MEAL PLAN ★ GROCERY SHOP AND FILL GAS TANK ★ MEAL PREP ★

DATE :

CLEANING CHEEKLIST

KEEP A GOOD THING GOING

EVERYDAY

	S	M	T	W	T	F	S
ONE LOAD OF LAUNDRY	◆	◆	◆	◆	◆	◆	◆
DISHES	◆	◆	◆	◆	◆	◆	◆
MAKE BEDS	◆	◆	◆	◆	◆	◆	◆
SPARY COUNTERTOPS	◆	◆	◆	◆	◆	◆	◆
PICK UP CLUTTER	◆	◆	◆	◆	◆	◆	◆
TRASH	◆	◆	◆	◆	◆	◆	◆
SORT MAIL	◆	◆	◆	◆	◆	◆	◆

MONTHLY

- ⬢ DUST CEILING FANS
- ⬢ CLEAN OVEN
- ⬢ CLEAN INSIDE OF FRIDGE
- ⬢ WASH WINDOWS
- ⬢ PICK UP GARAGE
- ⬢ PICK UP BASEMENT
- ⬢ DUST/CLEAN BASEBOARDS
- ⬢ GET RID OF ITEMS NO LONGER NEED
- ⬢ ------------------------------
- ⬢ ------------------------------
- ⬢ ------------------------------
- ⬢

MON — KITCHEN
- ★ CLEAN KITCHEN TABLE
- ★ WIPE DOWN SINK AND COUNTERS
- ★ VACUUM OR MOP
- ★ WIPE DOWN APPLIANCES
- ★

TUES — LIVINGROOM
- ★ PICK UP CLUTTER
- ★ VACUUM OR MOP
- ★ WASH BLANKETS
- ★ DUST SURFACES
- ★

WED — BEDROOM
- ★ PUT AWAY CLOTHES/PICK UP CLUTTER
- ★ DUST SURFACES
- ★ WASH BEDDING
- ★ VACUUM OR MOP
- ★

THUR — BATHROOM
- ★ SANITIZE TOILET
- ★ VACUUM OR MOP
- ★ WASH SHOWER,SINK AND MIRRORS
- ★ WASH TOWELS AND MATS
- ★

FRI — DINING
- ★ CLEAN OFF TABLE
- ★ VACUUM OR MOP
- ★ DUST SURFACES
- ★ PICK UP CLUTTER

SAT — ENTRY
- ★ SANTIZE DOORKNOBS
- ★ DUST SURFACES
- ★ VACUUM OR MOP
- ★ PUT AWAY SHOES/COATS/HATS
- ★

SUN — GROCERY
- ★ CLEAN OUT FRIDGE
- ★ MEAL PLAN
- ★ GROCERY SHOP AND FILL GAS TANK
- ★ MEAL PREP

DATE :

CLEANING CHEEKLIST

KEEP A GOOD THING GOING

EVERYDAY

	S	M	T	W	T	F	S
ONE LOAD OF LAUNDRY	◆	◆	◆	◆	◆	◆	◆
DISHES	◆	◆	◆	◆	◆	◆	◆
MAKE BEDS	◆	◆	◆	◆	◆	◆	◆
SPARY COUNTERTOPS	◆	◆	◆	◆	◆	◆	◆
PICK UP CLUTTER	◆	◆	◆	◆	◆	◆	◆
TRASH	◆	◆	◆	◆	◆	◆	◆
SORT MAIL	◆	◆	◆	◆	◆	◆	◆

MONTHLY

- DUST CEILING FANS
- CLEAN OVEN
- CLEAN INSIDE OF FRIDGE
- WASH WINDOWS
- PICK UP GARAGE
- PICK UP BASEMENT
- DUST/CLEAN BASEBOARDS
- GET RID OF ITEMS NO LONGER NEED
- -------------------------
- -------------------------
- -------------------------
-

MON	KITCHEN	⭐ CLEAN KITCHEN TABLE ⭐ WIPE DOWN SINK AND COUNTERS ⭐ VACUUM OR MOP ⭐ WIPE DOWN APPLIANCES ⭐
TUES	LIVINGROOM	⭐ PICK UP CLUTTER ⭐ VACUUM OR MOP ⭐ WASH BLANKETS ⭐ DUST SURFACES ⭐
WED	BEDROOM	⭐ PUT AWAY CLOTHES/PICK UP CLUTTER ⭐ DUST SURFACES ⭐ WASH BEDDING ⭐ VACUUM OR MOP ⭐
THUR	BATHROOM	⭐ SANITIZE TOILET ⭐ VACUUM OR MOP ⭐ WASH SHOWER,SINK AND MIRRORS ⭐ WASH TOWELS AND MATS ⭐
FRI	DINING	⭐ CLEAN OFF TABLE ⭐ VACUUM OR MOP ⭐ DUST SURFACES ⭐ PICK UP CLUTTER ⭐
SAT	ENTRY	⭐ SANTIZE DOORKNOBS ⭐ DUST SURFACES ⭐ VACUUM OR MOP ⭐ PUT AWAY SHOES/COATS/HATS ⭐
SUN	GROCERY	⭐ CLEAN OUT FRIDGE ⭐ MEAL PLAN ⭐ GROCERY SHOP AND FILL GAS TANK ⭐ MEAL PREP ⭐

DATE :

CLEANING CHEEKLIST

KEEP A GOOD THING GOING

EVERYDAY

	S	M	T	W	T	F	S
ONE LOAD OF LAUNDRY	◆	◆	◆	◆	◆	◆	◆
DISHES	◆	◆	◆	◆	◆	◆	◆
MAKE BEDS	◆	◆	◆	◆	◆	◆	◆
SPARY COUNTERTOPS	◆	◆	◆	◆	◆	◆	◆
PICK UP CLUTTER	◆	◆	◆	◆	◆	◆	◆
TRASH	◆	◆	◆	◆	◆	◆	◆
SORT MAIL	◆	◆	◆	◆	◆	◆	◆

MONTHLY

- ⬡ DUST CEILING FANS
- ⬡ CLEAN OVEN
- ⬡ CLEAN INSIDE OF FRIDGE
- ⬡ WASH WINDOWS
- ⬡ PICK UP GARAGE
- ⬡ PICK UP BASEMENT
- ⬡ DUST/CLEAN BASEBOARDS
- ⬡ GET RID OF ITEMS NO LONGER NEED
- ⬡ -----------------------------
- ⬡ -----------------------------
- ⬡ -----------------------------
- ⬡

MON	KITCHEN	☆ CLEAN KITCHEN TABLE
		☆ WIPE DOWN SINK AND COUNTERS
		☆ VACUUM OR MOP
		☆ WIPE DOWN APPLIANCES
		☆

TUES	LIVINGROOM	☆ PICK UP CLUTTER
		☆ VACUUM OR MOP
		☆ WASH BLANKETS
		☆ DUST SURFACES
		☆

WED	BEDROOM	☆ PUT AWAY CLOTHES/PICK UP CLUTTER
		☆ DUST SURFACES
		☆ WASH BEDDING
		☆ VACUUM OR MOP
		☆

THUR	BATHROOM	☆ SANITIZE TOILET
		☆ VACUUM OR MOP
		☆ WASH SHOWER,SINK AND MIRRORS
		☆ WASH TOWELS AND MATS
		☆

FRI	DINING	☆ CLEAN OFF TABLE
		☆ VACUUM OR MOP
		☆ DUST SURFACES
		☆ PICK UP CLUTTER
		☆

SAT	ENTRY	☆ SANTIZE DOORKNOBS
		☆ DUST SURFACES
		☆ VACUUM OR MOP
		☆ PUT AWAY SHOES/COATS/HATS
		☆

SUN	GROCERY	☆ CLEAN OUT FRIDGE
		☆ MEAL PLAN
		☆ GROCERY SHOP AND FILL GAS TANK
		☆ MEAL PREP
		☆

CLEANING CHEEKLIST

KEEP A GOOD THING GOING

EVERYDAY

	S	M	T	W	T	F	S
ONE LOAD OF LAUNDRY	◆	◆	◆	◆	◆	◆	◆
DISHES	◆	◆	◆	◆	◆	◆	◆
MAKE BEDS	◆	◆	◆	◆	◆	◆	◆
SPARY COUNTERTOPS	◆	◆	◆	◆	◆	◆	◆
PICK UP CLUTTER	◆	◆	◆	◆	◆	◆	◆
TRASH	◆	◆	◆	◆	◆	◆	◆
SORT MAIL	◆	◆	◆	◆	◆	◆	◆

MONTHLY

- DUST CEILING FANS
- CLEAN OVEN
- CLEAN INSIDE OF FRIDGE
- WASH WINDOWS
- PICK UP GARAGE
- PICK UP BASEMENT
- DUST/CLEAN BASEBOARDS
- GET RID OF ITEMS NO LONGER NEED
- _____
- _____
- _____
- _____

MON — KITCHEN
- ★ CLEAN KITCHEN TABLE
- ★ WIPE DOWN SINK AND COUNTERS
- ★ VACUUM OR MOP
- ★ WIPE DOWN APPLIANCES
- ★

TUES — LIVINGROOM
- ★ PICK UP CLUTTER
- ★ VACUUM OR MOP
- ★ WASH BLANKETS
- ★ DUST SURFACES
- ★

WED — BEDROOM
- ★ PUT AWAY CLOTHES/PICK UP CLUTTER
- ★ DUST SURFACES
- ★ WASH BEDDING
- ★ VACUUM OR MOP
- ★

THUR — BATHROOM
- ★ SANITIZE TOILET
- ★ VACUUM OR MOP
- ★ WASH SHOWER,SINK AND MIRRORS
- ★ WASH TOWELS AND MATS
- ★

FRI — DINING
- ★ CLEAN OFF TABLE
- ★ VACUUM OR MOP
- ★ DUST SURFACES
- ★ PICK UP CLUTTER
- ★

SAT — ENTRY
- ★ SANTIZE DOORKNOBS
- ★ DUST SURFACES
- ★ VACUUM OR MOP
- ★ PUT AWAY SHOES/COATS/HATS
- ★

SUN — GROCERY
- ★ CLEAN OUT FRIDGE
- ★ MEAL PLAN
- ★ GROCERY SHOP AND FILL GAS TANK
- ★ MEAL PREP
- ★

DATE :

CLEANING CHEEKLIST

KEEP A GOOD THING GOING

EVERYDAY

	S	M	T	W	T	F	S
ONE LOAD OF LAUNDRY	◆	◆	◆	◆	◆	◆	◆
DISHES	◆	◆	◆	◆	◆	◆	◆
MAKE BEDS	◆	◆	◆	◆	◆	◆	◆
SPARY COUNTERTOPS	◆	◆	◆	◆	◆	◆	◆
PICK UP CLUTTER	◆	◆	◆	◆	◆	◆	◆
TRASH	◆	◆	◆	◆	◆	◆	◆
SORT MAIL	◆	◆	◆	◆	◆	◆	◆

MONTHLY

- DUST CEILING FANS
- CLEAN OVEN
- CLEAN INSIDE OF FRIDGE
- WASH WINDOWS
- PICK UP GARAGE
- PICK UP BASEMENT
- DUST/CLEAN BASEBOARDS
- GET RID OF ITEMS NO LONGER NEED
- _____
- _____
- _____
- _____

MON — KITCHEN
- ★ CLEAN KITCHEN TABLE
- ★ WIPE DOWN SINK AND COUNTERS
- ★ VACUUM OR MOP
- ★ WIPE DOWN APPLIANCES
- ★

TUES — LIVINGROOM
- ★ PICK UP CLUTTER
- ★ VACUUM OR MOP
- ★ WASH BLANKETS
- ★ DUST SURFACES
- ★

WED — BEDROOM
- ★ PUT AWAY CLOTHES/PICK UP CLUTTER
- ★ DUST SURFACES
- ★ WASH BEDDING
- ★ VACUUM OR MOP
- ★

THUR — BATHROOM
- ★ SANITIZE TOILET
- ★ VACUUM OR MOP
- ★ WASH SHOWER, SINK AND MIRRORS
- ★ WASH TOWELS AND MATS
- ★

FRI — DINING
- ★ CLEAN OFF TABLE
- ★ VACUUM OR MOP
- ★ DUST SURFACES
- ★ PICK UP CLUTTER
- ★

SAT — ENTRY
- ★ SANTIZE DOORKNOBS
- ★ DUST SURFACES
- ★ VACUUM OR MOP
- ★ PUT AWAY SHOES/COATS/HATS
- ★

SUN — GROCERY
- ★ CLEAN OUT FRIDGE
- ★ MEAL PLAN
- ★ GROCERY SHOP AND FILL GAS TANK
- ★ MEAL PREP
- ★

DATE :

CLEANING CHECKLIST

KEEP A GOOD THING GOING

EVERYDAY

	S	M	T	W	T	F	S
ONE LOAD OF LAUNDRY	◆	◆	◆	◆	◆	◆	◆
DISHES	◆	◆	◆	◆	◆	◆	◆
MAKE BEDS	◆	◆	◆	◆	◆	◆	◆
SPARY COUNTERTOPS	◆	◆	◆	◆	◆	◆	◆
PICK UP CLUTTER	◆	◆	◆	◆	◆	◆	◆
TRASH	◆	◆	◆	◆	◆	◆	◆
SORT MAIL	◆	◆	◆	◆	◆	◆	◆

MONTHLY

- DUST CEILING FANS
- CLEAN OVEN
- CLEAN INSIDE OF FRIDGE
- WASH WINDOWS
- PICK UP GARAGE
- PICK UP BASEMENT
- DUST/CLEAN BASEBOARDS
- GET RID OF ITEMS NO LONGER NEED
- ------------------------------
- ------------------------------
- ------------------------------
- ------------------------------

MON — KITCHEN
- ★ CLEAN KITCHEN TABLE
- ★ WIPE DOWN SINK AND COUNTERS
- ★ VACUUM OR MOP
- ★ WIPE DOWN APPLIANCES
- ★

TUES — LIVINGROOM
- ★ PICK UP CLUTTER
- ★ VACUUM OR MOP
- ★ WASH BLANKETS
- ★ DUST SURFACES
- ★

WED — BEDROOM
- ★ PUT AWAY CLOTHES/PICK UP CLUTTER
- ★ DUST SURFACES
- ★ WASH BEDDING
- ★ VACUUM OR MOP
- ★

THUR — BATHROOM
- ★ SANITIZE TOILET
- ★ VACUUM OR MOP
- ★ WASH SHOWER,SINK AND MIRRORS
- ★ WASH TOWELS AND MATS
- ★

FRI — DINING
- ★ CLEAN OFF TABLE
- ★ VACUUM OR MOP
- ★ DUST SURFACES
- ★ PICK UP CLUTTER
- ★

SAT — ENTRY
- ★ SANTIZE DOORKNOBS
- ★ DUST SURFACES
- ★ VACUUM OR MOP
- ★ PUT AWAY SHOES/COATS/HATS
- ★

SUN — GROCERY
- ★ CLEAN OUT FRIDGE
- ★ MEAL PLAN
- ★ GROCERY SHOP AND FILL GAS TANK
- ★ MEAL PREP
- ★

CLEANING CHEEKLIST

KEEP A GOOD THING GOING

EVERYDAY

	S	M	T	W	T	F	S
ONE LOAD OF LAUNDRY	◆	◆	◆	◆	◆	◆	◆
DISHES	◆	◆	◆	◆	◆	◆	◆
MAKE BEDS	◆	◆	◆	◆	◆	◆	◆
SPARY COUNTERTOPS	◆	◆	◆	◆	◆	◆	◆
PICK UP CLUTTER	◆	◆	◆	◆	◆	◆	◆
TRASH	◆	◆	◆	◆	◆	◆	◆
SORT MAIL	◆	◆	◆	◆	◆	◆	◆

MONTHLY

- DUST CEILING FANS
- CLEAN OVEN
- CLEAN INSIDE OF FRIDGE
- WASH WINDOWS
- PICK UP GARAGE
- PICK UP BASEMENT
- DUST/CLEAN BASEBOARDS
- GET RID OF ITEMS NO LONGER NEED
- _____
- _____
- _____
- _____

MON — KITCHEN
- ★ CLEAN KITCHEN TABLE
- ★ WIPE DOWN SINK AND COUNTERS
- ★ VACUUM OR MOP
- ★ WIPE DOWN APPLIANCES
- ★

TUES — LIVINGROOM
- ★ PICK UP CLUTTER
- ★ VACUUM OR MOP
- ★ WASH BLANKETS
- ★ DUST SURFACES
- ★

WED — BEDROOM
- ★ PUT AWAY CLOTHES/PICK UP CLUTTER
- ★ DUST SURFACES
- ★ WASH BEDDING
- ★ VACUUM OR MOP
- ★

THUR — BATHROOM
- ★ SANITIZE TOILET
- ★ VACUUM OR MOP
- ★ WASH SHOWER,SINK AND MIRRORS
- ★ WASH TOWELS AND MATS
- ★

FRI — DINING
- ★ CLEAN OFF TABLE
- ★ VACUUM OR MOP
- ★ DUST SURFACES
- ★ PICK UP CLUTTER
- ★

SAT — ENTRY
- ★ SANTIZE DOORKNOBS
- ★ DUST SURFACES
- ★ VACUUM OR MOP
- ★ PUT AWAY SHOES/COATS/HATS
- ★

SUN — GROCERY
- ★ CLEAN OUT FRIDGE
- ★ MEAL PLAN
- ★ GROCERY SHOP AND FILL GAS TANK
- ★ MEAL PREP
- ★

DATE :

CLEANING CHEEKLIST

KEEP A GOOD THING GOING

EVERYDAY

	S	M	T	W	T	F	S
ONE LOAD OF LAUNDRY	◆	◆	◆	◆	◆	◆	◆
DISHES	◆	◆	◆	◆	◆	◆	◆
MAKE BEDS	◆	◆	◆	◆	◆	◆	◆
SPARY COUNTERTOPS	◆	◆	◆	◆	◆	◆	◆
PICK UP CLUTTER	◆	◆	◆	◆	◆	◆	◆
TRASH	◆	◆	◆	◆	◆	◆	◆
SORT MAIL	◆	◆	◆	◆	◆	◆	◆

MONTHLY

- ⬡ DUST CEILING FANS
- ⬡ CLEAN OVEN
- ⬡ CLEAN INSIDE OF FRIDGE
- ⬡ WASH WINDOWS
- ⬡ PICK UP GARAGE
- ⬡ PICK UP BASEMENT
- ⬡ DUST/CLEAN BASEBOARDS
- ⬡ GET RID OF ITEMS NO LONGER NEED
- ⬡ -
- ⬡ -
- ⬡ -
- ⬡ -

MON	KITCHEN	★ CLEAN KITCHEN TABLE ★ WIPE DOWN SINK AND COUNTERS ★ VACUUM OR MOP ★ WIPE DOWN APPLIANCES ★
TUES	LIVING ROOM	★ PICK UP CLUTTER ★ VACUUM OR MOP ★ WASH BLANKETS ★ DUST SURFACES ★
WED	BEDROOM	★ PUT AWAY CLOTHES/PICK UP CLUTTER ★ DUST SURFACES ★ WASH BEDDING ★ VACUUM OR MOP ★
THUR	BATHROOM	★ SANITIZE TOILET ★ VACUUM OR MOP ★ WASH SHOWER,SINK AND MIRRORS ★ WASH TOWELS AND MATS ★
FRI	DINING	★ CLEAN OFF TABLE ★ VACUUM OR MOP ★ DUST SURFACES ★ PICK UP CLUTTER ★
SAT	ENTRY	★ SANTIZE DOORKNOBS ★ DUST SURFACES ★ VACUUM OR MOP ★ PUT AWAY SHOES/COATS/HATS ★
SUN	GROCERY	★ CLEAN OUT FRIDGE ★ MEAL PLAN ★ GROCERY SHOP AND FILL GAS TANK ★ MEAL PREP ★

DATE :   CLEANING CHEEKLIST

KEEP A GOOD THING GOING

EVERYDAY

	S	M	T	W	T	F	S
ONE LOAD OF LAUNDRY	◆	◆	◆	◆	◆	◆	◆
DISHES	◆	◆	◆	◆	◆	◆	◆
MAKE BEDS	◆	◆	◆	◆	◆	◆	◆
SPARY COUNTERTOPS	◆	◆	◆	◆	◆	◆	◆
PICK UP CLUTTER	◆	◆	◆	◆	◆	◆	◆
TRASH	◆	◆	◆	◆	◆	◆	◆
SORT MAIL	◆	◆	◆	◆	◆	◆	◆

MONTHLY

- ⬡ DUST CEILING FANS
- ⬡ CLEAN OVEN
- ⬡ CLEAN INSIDE OF FRIDGE
- ⬡ WASH WINDOWS
- ⬡ PICK UP GARAGE
- ⬡ PICK UP BASEMENT
- ⬡ DUST/CLEAN BASEBOARDS
- ⬡ GET RID OF ITEMS NO LONGER NEED
- ⬡ ------------------------------
- ⬡ ------------------------------
- ⬡ ------------------------------
- ⬡ ------------------------------

MON	**KITCHEN**	★ CLEAN KITCHEN TABLE ★ WIPE DOWN SINK AND COUNTERS ★ VACUUM OR MOP ★ WIPE DOWN APPLIANCES ★
TUES	**LIVING ROOM**	★ PICK UP CLUTTER ★ VACUUM OR MOP ★ WASH BLANKETS ★ DUST SURFACES ★
WED	**BEDROOM**	★ PUT AWAY CLOTHES/PICK UP CLUTTER ★ DUST SURFACES ★ WASH BEDDING ★ VACUUM OR MOP ★
THUR	**BATHROOM**	★ SANITIZE TOILET ★ VACUUM OR MOP ★ WASH SHOWER,SINK AND MIRRORS ★ WASH TOWELS AND MATS ★
FRI	**DINING**	★ CLEAN OFF TABLE ★ VACUUM OR MOP ★ DUST SURFACES ★ PICK UP CLUTTER ★
SAT	**ENTRY**	★ SANTIZE DOORKNOBS ★ DUST SURFACES ★ VACUUM OR MOP ★ PUT AWAY SHOES/COATS/HATS ★
SUN	**GROCERY**	★ CLEAN OUT FRIDGE ★ MEAL PLAN ★ GROCERY SHOP AND FILL GAS TANK ★ MEAL PREP ★

DATE :

CLEANING CHEEKLIST

KEEP A GOOD THING GOING

EVERYDAY

	S	M	T	W	T	F	S
ONE LOAD OF LAUNDRY	◆	◆	◆	◆	◆	◆	◆
DISHES	◆	◆	◆	◆	◆	◆	◆
MAKE BEDS	◆	◆	◆	◆	◆	◆	◆
SPARY COUNTERTOPS	◆	◆	◆	◆	◆	◆	◆
PICK UP CLUTTER	◆	◆	◆	◆	◆	◆	◆
TRASH	◆	◆	◆	◆	◆	◆	◆
SORT MAIL	◆	◆	◆	◆	◆	◆	◆

MONTHLY

- DUST CEILING FANS
- CLEAN OVEN
- CLEAN INSIDE OF FRIDGE
- WASH WINDOWS
- PICK UP GARAGE
- PICK UP BASEMENT
- DUST/CLEAN BASEBOARDS
- GET RID OF ITEMS NO LONGER NEED
- -
- -
- -
- -

MON	KITCHEN	☆ CLEAN KITCHEN TABLE ☆ WIPE DOWN SINK AND COUNTERS ☆ VACUUM OR MOP ☆ WIPE DOWN APPLIANCES ☆
TUES	LIVINGROOM	☆ PICK UP CLUTTER ☆ VACUUM OR MOP ☆ WASH BLANKETS ☆ DUST SURFACES ☆
WED	BEDROOM	☆ PUT AWAY CLOTHES/PICK UP CLUTTER ☆ DUST SURFACES ☆ WASH BEDDING ☆ VACUUM OR MOP ☆
THUR	BATHROOM	☆ SANITIZE TOILET ☆ VACUUM OR MOP ☆ WASH SHOWER,SINK AND MIRRORS ☆ WASH TOWELS AND MATS ☆
FRI	DINING	☆ CLEAN OFF TABLE ☆ VACUUM OR MOP ☆ DUST SURFACES ☆ PICK UP CLUTTER ☆
SAT	ENTRY	☆ SANTIZE DOORKNOBS ☆ DUST SURFACES ☆ VACUUM OR MOP ☆ PUT AWAY SHOES/COATS/HATS ☆
SUN	GROCERY	☆ CLEAN OUT FRIDGE ☆ MEAL PLAN ☆ GROCERY SHOP AND FILL GAS TANK ☆ MEAL PREP ☆

DATE :

CLEANING CHEEKLIST

KEEP A GOOD THING GOING

EVERYDAY

	S	M	T	W	T	F	S
ONE LOAD OF LAUNDRY	◆	◆	◆	◆	◆	◆	◆
DISHES	◆	◆	◆	◆	◆	◆	◆
MAKE BEDS	◆	◆	◆	◆	◆	◆	◆
SPARY COUNTERTOPS	◆	◆	◆	◆	◆	◆	◆
PICK UP CLUTTER	◆	◆	◆	◆	◆	◆	◆
TRASH	◆	◆	◆	◆	◆	◆	◆
SORT MAIL	◆	◆	◆	◆	◆	◆	◆

MONTHLY

- DUST CEILING FANS
- CLEAN OVEN
- CLEAN INSIDE OF FRIDGE
- WASH WINDOWS
- PICK UP GARAGE
- PICK UP BASEMENT
- DUST/CLEAN BASEBOARDS
- GET RID OF ITEMS NO LONGER NEED
- --------------------------------
- --------------------------------
- --------------------------------
-

MON — **KITCHEN**
- ★ CLEAN KITCHEN TABLE
- ★ WIPE DOWN SINK AND COUNTERS
- ★ VACUUM OR MOP
- ★ WIPE DOWN APPLIANCES
- ★

TUES — **LIVINGROOM**
- ★ PICK UP CLUTTER
- ★ VACUUM OR MOP
- ★ WASH BLANKETS
- ★ DUST SURFACES
- ★

WED — **BEDROOM**
- ★ PUT AWAY CLOTHES/PICK UP CLUTTER
- ★ DUST SURFACES
- ★ WASH BEDDING
- ★ VACUUM OR MOP
- ★

THUR — **BATHROOM**
- ★ SANITIZE TOILET
- ★ VACUUM OR MOP
- ★ WASH SHOWER,SINK AND MIRRORS
- ★ WASH TOWELS AND MATS
- ★

FRI — **DINING**
- ★ CLEAN OFF TABLE
- ★ VACUUM OR MOP
- ★ DUST SURFACES
- ★ PICK UP CLUTTER
- ★

SAT — **ENTRY**
- ★ SANTIZE DOORKNOBS
- ★ DUST SURFACES
- ★ VACUUM OR MOP
- ★ PUT AWAY SHOES/COATS/HATS
- ★

SUN — **GROCERY**
- ★ CLEAN OUT FRIDGE
- ★ MEAL PLAN
- ★ GROCERY SHOP AND FILL GAS TANK
- ★ MEAL PREP
- ★

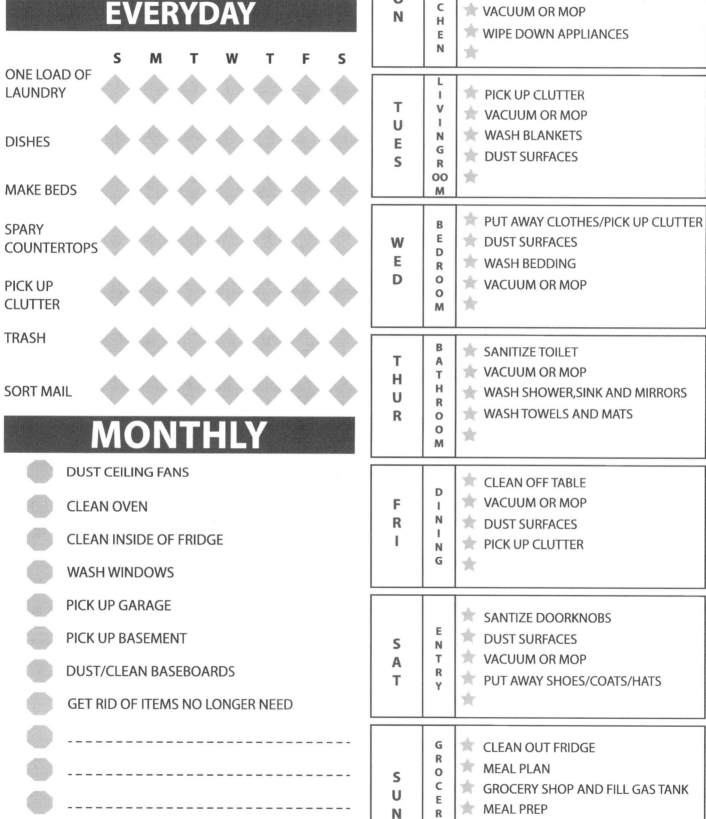

CLEANING CHEEKLIST

DATE :

KEEP A GOOD THING GOING

EVERYDAY

	S	M	T	W	T	F	S
ONE LOAD OF LAUNDRY	◆	◆	◆	◆	◆	◆	◆
DISHES	◆	◆	◆	◆	◆	◆	◆
MAKE BEDS	◆	◆	◆	◆	◆	◆	◆
SPARY COUNTERTOPS	◆	◆	◆	◆	◆	◆	◆
PICK UP CLUTTER	◆	◆	◆	◆	◆	◆	◆
TRASH	◆	◆	◆	◆	◆	◆	◆
SORT MAIL	◆	◆	◆	◆	◆	◆	◆

MONTHLY

- ⬡ DUST CEILING FANS
- ⬡ CLEAN OVEN
- ⬡ CLEAN INSIDE OF FRIDGE
- ⬡ WASH WINDOWS
- ⬡ PICK UP GARAGE
- ⬡ PICK UP BASEMENT
- ⬡ DUST/CLEAN BASEBOARDS
- ⬡ GET RID OF ITEMS NO LONGER NEED
- ⬡ _____
- ⬡ _____
- ⬡ _____
- ⬡ _____

MON	KITCHEN	★ CLEAN KITCHEN TABLE ★ WIPE DOWN SINK AND COUNTERS ★ VACUUM OR MOP ★ WIPE DOWN APPLIANCES ★
TUES	LIVING ROOM	★ PICK UP CLUTTER ★ VACUUM OR MOP ★ WASH BLANKETS ★ DUST SURFACES ★
WED	BEDROOM	★ PUT AWAY CLOTHES/PICK UP CLUTTER ★ DUST SURFACES ★ WASH BEDDING ★ VACUUM OR MOP ★
THUR	BATHROOM	★ SANITIZE TOILET ★ VACUUM OR MOP ★ WASH SHOWER,SINK AND MIRRORS ★ WASH TOWELS AND MATS ★
FRI	DINING	★ CLEAN OFF TABLE ★ VACUUM OR MOP ★ DUST SURFACES ★ PICK UP CLUTTER ★
SAT	ENTRY	★ SANTIZE DOORKNOBS ★ DUST SURFACES ★ VACUUM OR MOP ★ PUT AWAY SHOES/COATS/HATS ★
SUN	GROCERY	★ CLEAN OUT FRIDGE ★ MEAL PLAN ★ GROCERY SHOP AND FILL GAS TANK ★ MEAL PREP ★

DATE :   CLEANING CHEEKLIST

KEEP A GOOD THING GOING

EVERYDAY

	S	M	T	W	T	F	S
ONE LOAD OF LAUNDRY	◆	◆	◆	◆	◆	◆	◆
DISHES	◆	◆	◆	◆	◆	◆	◆
MAKE BEDS	◆	◆	◆	◆	◆	◆	◆
SPARY COUNTERTOPS	◆	◆	◆	◆	◆	◆	◆
PICK UP CLUTTER	◆	◆	◆	◆	◆	◆	◆
TRASH	◆	◆	◆	◆	◆	◆	◆
SORT MAIL	◆	◆	◆	◆	◆	◆	◆

MONTHLY

- ⬡ DUST CEILING FANS
- ⬡ CLEAN OVEN
- ⬡ CLEAN INSIDE OF FRIDGE
- ⬡ WASH WINDOWS
- ⬡ PICK UP GARAGE
- ⬡ PICK UP BASEMENT
- ⬡ DUST/CLEAN BASEBOARDS
- ⬡ GET RID OF ITEMS NO LONGER NEED
- ⬡ -------------------------------
- ⬡ -------------------------------
- ⬡ -------------------------------
- ⬡ -------------------------------

MON	KITCHEN	☆ CLEAN KITCHEN TABLE ☆ WIPE DOWN SINK AND COUNTERS ☆ VACUUM OR MOP ☆ WIPE DOWN APPLIANCES ☆
TUES	LIVINGROOM	☆ PICK UP CLUTTER ☆ VACUUM OR MOP ☆ WASH BLANKETS ☆ DUST SURFACES ☆
WED	BEDROOM	☆ PUT AWAY CLOTHES/PICK UP CLUTTER ☆ DUST SURFACES ☆ WASH BEDDING ☆ VACUUM OR MOP ☆
THUR	BATHROOM	☆ SANITIZE TOILET ☆ VACUUM OR MOP ☆ WASH SHOWER,SINK AND MIRRORS ☆ WASH TOWELS AND MATS ☆
FRI	DINING	☆ CLEAN OFF TABLE ☆ VACUUM OR MOP ☆ DUST SURFACES ☆ PICK UP CLUTTER ☆
SAT	ENTRY	☆ SANTIZE DOORKNOBS ☆ DUST SURFACES ☆ VACUUM OR MOP ☆ PUT AWAY SHOES/COATS/HATS ☆
SUN	GROCERY	☆ CLEAN OUT FRIDGE ☆ MEAL PLAN ☆ GROCERY SHOP AND FILL GAS TANK ☆ MEAL PREP ☆

DATE :   CLEANING CHEEKLIST

KEEP A GOOD THING GOING

EVERYDAY

	S	M	T	W	T	F	S
ONE LOAD OF LAUNDRY	◆	◆	◆	◆	◆	◆	◆
DISHES	◆	◆	◆	◆	◆	◆	◆
MAKE BEDS	◆	◆	◆	◆	◆	◆	◆
SPARY COUNTERTOPS	◆	◆	◆	◆	◆	◆	◆
PICK UP CLUTTER	◆	◆	◆	◆	◆	◆	◆
TRASH	◆	◆	◆	◆	◆	◆	◆
SORT MAIL	◆	◆	◆	◆	◆	◆	◆

MONTHLY

- DUST CEILING FANS
- CLEAN OVEN
- CLEAN INSIDE OF FRIDGE
- WASH WINDOWS
- PICK UP GARAGE
- PICK UP BASEMENT
- DUST/CLEAN BASEBOARDS
- GET RID OF ITEMS NO LONGER NEED
- _____
- _____
- _____
- _____

MON — KITCHEN
- ★ CLEAN KITCHEN TABLE
- ★ WIPE DOWN SINK AND COUNTERS
- ★ VACUUM OR MOP
- ★ WIPE DOWN APPLIANCES
- ★

TUES — LIVING ROOM
- ★ PICK UP CLUTTER
- ★ VACUUM OR MOP
- ★ WASH BLANKETS
- ★ DUST SURFACES
- ★

WED — BEDROOM
- ★ PUT AWAY CLOTHES/PICK UP CLUTTER
- ★ DUST SURFACES
- ★ WASH BEDDING
- ★ VACUUM OR MOP
- ★

THUR — BATHROOM
- ★ SANITIZE TOILET
- ★ VACUUM OR MOP
- ★ WASH SHOWER,SINK AND MIRRORS
- ★ WASH TOWELS AND MATS
- ★

FRI — DINING
- ★ CLEAN OFF TABLE
- ★ VACUUM OR MOP
- ★ DUST SURFACES
- ★ PICK UP CLUTTER
- ★

SAT — ENTRY
- ★ SANTIZE DOORKNOBS
- ★ DUST SURFACES
- ★ VACUUM OR MOP
- ★ PUT AWAY SHOES/COATS/HATS
- ★

SUN — GROCERY
- ★ CLEAN OUT FRIDGE
- ★ MEAL PLAN
- ★ GROCERY SHOP AND FILL GAS TANK
- ★ MEAL PREP
- ★

DATE :

CLEANING CHEEKLIST

KEEP A GOOD THING GOING

EVERYDAY

	S	M	T	W	T	F	S
ONE LOAD OF LAUNDRY	◆	◆	◆	◆	◆	◆	◆
DISHES	◆	◆	◆	◆	◆	◆	◆
MAKE BEDS	◆	◆	◆	◆	◆	◆	◆
SPARY COUNTERTOPS	◆	◆	◆	◆	◆	◆	◆
PICK UP CLUTTER	◆	◆	◆	◆	◆	◆	◆
TRASH	◆	◆	◆	◆	◆	◆	◆
SORT MAIL	◆	◆	◆	◆	◆	◆	◆

MONTHLY

- DUST CEILING FANS
- CLEAN OVEN
- CLEAN INSIDE OF FRIDGE
- WASH WINDOWS
- PICK UP GARAGE
- PICK UP BASEMENT
- DUST/CLEAN BASEBOARDS
- GET RID OF ITEMS NO LONGER NEED
- ------------------------
- ------------------------
- ------------------------
- ------------------------

MON	KITCHEN	☆ CLEAN KITCHEN TABLE
		☆ WIPE DOWN SINK AND COUNTERS
		☆ VACUUM OR MOP
		☆ WIPE DOWN APPLIANCES
		☆

TUES	LIVINGROOM	☆ PICK UP CLUTTER
		☆ VACUUM OR MOP
		☆ WASH BLANKETS
		☆ DUST SURFACES
		☆

WED	BEDROOM	☆ PUT AWAY CLOTHES/PICK UP CLUTTER
		☆ DUST SURFACES
		☆ WASH BEDDING
		☆ VACUUM OR MOP
		☆

THUR	BATHROOM	☆ SANITIZE TOILET
		☆ VACUUM OR MOP
		☆ WASH SHOWER,SINK AND MIRRORS
		☆ WASH TOWELS AND MATS
		☆

FRI	DINING	☆ CLEAN OFF TABLE
		☆ VACUUM OR MOP
		☆ DUST SURFACES
		☆ PICK UP CLUTTER
		☆

SAT	ENTRY	☆ SANTIZE DOORKNOBS
		☆ DUST SURFACES
		☆ VACUUM OR MOP
		☆ PUT AWAY SHOES/COATS/HATS
		☆

SUN	GROCERY	☆ CLEAN OUT FRIDGE
		☆ MEAL PLAN
		☆ GROCERY SHOP AND FILL GAS TANK
		☆ MEAL PREP
		☆

DATE :

CLEANING CHEEKLIST

KEEP A GOOD THING GOING

EVERYDAY

	S	M	T	W	T	F	S
ONE LOAD OF LAUNDRY	◆	◆	◆	◆	◆	◆	◆
DISHES	◆	◆	◆	◆	◆	◆	◆
MAKE BEDS	◆	◆	◆	◆	◆	◆	◆
SPARY COUNTERTOPS	◆	◆	◆	◆	◆	◆	◆
PICK UP CLUTTER	◆	◆	◆	◆	◆	◆	◆
TRASH	◆	◆	◆	◆	◆	◆	◆
SORT MAIL	◆	◆	◆	◆	◆	◆	◆

MONTHLY

- ⬡ DUST CEILING FANS
- ⬡ CLEAN OVEN
- ⬡ CLEAN INSIDE OF FRIDGE
- ⬡ WASH WINDOWS
- ⬡ PICK UP GARAGE
- ⬡ PICK UP BASEMENT
- ⬡ DUST/CLEAN BASEBOARDS
- ⬡ GET RID OF ITEMS NO LONGER NEED
- ⬡ _____
- ⬡ _____
- ⬡ _____
- ⬡ _____

MON — KITCHEN
- ★ CLEAN KITCHEN TABLE
- ★ WIPE DOWN SINK AND COUNTERS
- ★ VACUUM OR MOP
- ★ WIPE DOWN APPLIANCES
- ★

TUES — LIVINGROOM
- ★ PICK UP CLUTTER
- ★ VACUUM OR MOP
- ★ WASH BLANKETS
- ★ DUST SURFACES
- ★

WED — BEDROOM
- ★ PUT AWAY CLOTHES/PICK UP CLUTTER
- ★ DUST SURFACES
- ★ WASH BEDDING
- ★ VACUUM OR MOP
- ★

THUR — BATHROOM
- ★ SANITIZE TOILET
- ★ VACUUM OR MOP
- ★ WASH SHOWER,SINK AND MIRRORS
- ★ WASH TOWELS AND MATS
- ★

FRI — DINING
- ★ CLEAN OFF TABLE
- ★ VACUUM OR MOP
- ★ DUST SURFACES
- ★ PICK UP CLUTTER
- ★

SAT — ENTRY
- ★ SANTIZE DOORKNOBS
- ★ DUST SURFACES
- ★ VACUUM OR MOP
- ★ PUT AWAY SHOES/COATS/HATS
- ★

SUN — GROCERY
- ★ CLEAN OUT FRIDGE
- ★ MEAL PLAN
- ★ GROCERY SHOP AND FILL GAS TANK
- ★ MEAL PREP

DATE:

CLEANING CHEEKLIST

KEEP A GOOD THING GOING

EVERYDAY

	S	M	T	W	T	F	S
ONE LOAD OF LAUNDRY	◆	◆	◆	◆	◆	◆	◆
DISHES	◆	◆	◆	◆	◆	◆	◆
MAKE BEDS	◆	◆	◆	◆	◆	◆	◆
SPARY COUNTERTOPS	◆	◆	◆	◆	◆	◆	◆
PICK UP CLUTTER	◆	◆	◆	◆	◆	◆	◆
TRASH	◆	◆	◆	◆	◆	◆	◆
SORT MAIL	◆	◆	◆	◆	◆	◆	◆

MONTHLY

- ⬡ DUST CEILING FANS
- ⬡ CLEAN OVEN
- ⬡ CLEAN INSIDE OF FRIDGE
- ⬡ WASH WINDOWS
- ⬡ PICK UP GARAGE
- ⬡ PICK UP BASEMENT
- ⬡ DUST/CLEAN BASEBOARDS
- ⬡ GET RID OF ITEMS NO LONGER NEED
- ⬡ -----------------------------
- ⬡ -----------------------------
- ⬡ -----------------------------
- ⬡ -----------------------------

MON	KITCHEN	☆ CLEAN KITCHEN TABLE
		☆ WIPE DOWN SINK AND COUNTERS
		☆ VACUUM OR MOP
		☆ WIPE DOWN APPLIANCES
		☆

TUES	LIVINGROOM	☆ PICK UP CLUTTER
		☆ VACUUM OR MOP
		☆ WASH BLANKETS
		☆ DUST SURFACES
		☆

WED	BEDROOM	☆ PUT AWAY CLOTHES/PICK UP CLUTTER
		☆ DUST SURFACES
		☆ WASH BEDDING
		☆ VACUUM OR MOP
		☆

THUR	BATHROOM	☆ SANITIZE TOILET
		☆ VACUUM OR MOP
		☆ WASH SHOWER,SINK AND MIRRORS
		☆ WASH TOWELS AND MATS
		☆

FRI	DINING	☆ CLEAN OFF TABLE
		☆ VACUUM OR MOP
		☆ DUST SURFACES
		☆ PICK UP CLUTTER
		☆

SAT	ENTRY	☆ SANTIZE DOORKNOBS
		☆ DUST SURFACES
		☆ VACUUM OR MOP
		☆ PUT AWAY SHOES/COATS/HATS
		☆

SUN	GROCERY	☆ CLEAN OUT FRIDGE
		☆ MEAL PLAN
		☆ GROCERY SHOP AND FILL GAS TANK
		☆ MEAL PREP
		☆

DATE :

CLEANING CHEEKLIST

KEEP A GOOD THING GOING

EVERYDAY

	S	M	T	W	T	F	S
ONE LOAD OF LAUNDRY	◆	◆	◆	◆	◆	◆	◆
DISHES	◆	◆	◆	◆	◆	◆	◆
MAKE BEDS	◆	◆	◆	◆	◆	◆	◆
SPARY COUNTERTOPS	◆	◆	◆	◆	◆	◆	◆
PICK UP CLUTTER	◆	◆	◆	◆	◆	◆	◆
TRASH	◆	◆	◆	◆	◆	◆	◆
SORT MAIL	◆	◆	◆	◆	◆	◆	◆

MONTHLY

- DUST CEILING FANS
- CLEAN OVEN
- CLEAN INSIDE OF FRIDGE
- WASH WINDOWS
- PICK UP GARAGE
- PICK UP BASEMENT
- DUST/CLEAN BASEBOARDS
- GET RID OF ITEMS NO LONGER NEED
- ------------------------------
- ------------------------------
- ------------------------------
- ------------------------------

MON — KITCHEN
- ★ CLEAN KITCHEN TABLE
- ★ WIPE DOWN SINK AND COUNTERS
- ★ VACUUM OR MOP
- ★ WIPE DOWN APPLIANCES
- ★

TUES — LIVINGROOM
- ★ PICK UP CLUTTER
- ★ VACUUM OR MOP
- ★ WASH BLANKETS
- ★ DUST SURFACES
- ★

WED — BEDROOM
- ★ PUT AWAY CLOTHES/PICK UP CLUTTER
- ★ DUST SURFACES
- ★ WASH BEDDING
- ★ VACUUM OR MOP
- ★

THUR — BATHROOM
- ★ SANITIZE TOILET
- ★ VACUUM OR MOP
- ★ WASH SHOWER,SINK AND MIRRORS
- ★ WASH TOWELS AND MATS
- ★

FRI — DINING
- ★ CLEAN OFF TABLE
- ★ VACUUM OR MOP
- ★ DUST SURFACES
- ★ PICK UP CLUTTER
- ★

SAT — ENTRY
- ★ SANTIZE DOORKNOBS
- ★ DUST SURFACES
- ★ VACUUM OR MOP
- ★ PUT AWAY SHOES/COATS/HATS
- ★

SUN — GROCERY
- ★ CLEAN OUT FRIDGE
- ★ MEAL PLAN
- ★ GROCERY SHOP AND FILL GAS TANK
- ★ MEAL PREP
- ★

KEEP A GOOD THING GOING

EVERYDAY

	S	M	T	W	T	F	S
ONE LOAD OF LAUNDRY	◆	◆	◆	◆	◆	◆	◆
DISHES	◆	◆	◆	◆	◆	◆	◆
MAKE BEDS	◆	◆	◆	◆	◆	◆	◆
SPARY COUNTERTOPS	◆	◆	◆	◆	◆	◆	◆
PICK UP CLUTTER	◆	◆	◆	◆	◆	◆	◆
TRASH	◆	◆	◆	◆	◆	◆	◆
SORT MAIL	◆	◆	◆	◆	◆	◆	◆

MONTHLY

- DUST CEILING FANS
- CLEAN OVEN
- CLEAN INSIDE OF FRIDGE
- WASH WINDOWS
- PICK UP GARAGE
- PICK UP BASEMENT
- DUST/CLEAN BASEBOARDS
- GET RID OF ITEMS NO LONGER NEED
- -------------------------------
- -------------------------------
- -------------------------------

MON	KITCHEN	★ CLEAN KITCHEN TABLE ★ WIPE DOWN SINK AND COUNTERS ★ VACUUM OR MOP ★ WIPE DOWN APPLIANCES ★
TUES	LIVINGROOM	★ PICK UP CLUTTER ★ VACUUM OR MOP ★ WASH BLANKETS ★ DUST SURFACES ★
WED	BEDROOM	★ PUT AWAY CLOTHES/PICK UP CLUTTER ★ DUST SURFACES ★ WASH BEDDING ★ VACUUM OR MOP ★
THUR	BATHROOM	★ SANITIZE TOILET ★ VACUUM OR MOP ★ WASH SHOWER,SINK AND MIRRORS ★ WASH TOWELS AND MATS ★
FRI	DINING	★ CLEAN OFF TABLE ★ VACUUM OR MOP ★ DUST SURFACES ★ PICK UP CLUTTER ★
SAT	ENTRY	★ SANTIZE DOORKNOBS ★ DUST SURFACES ★ VACUUM OR MOP ★ PUT AWAY SHOES/COATS/HATS ★
SUN	GROCERY	★ CLEAN OUT FRIDGE ★ MEAL PLAN ★ GROCERY SHOP AND FILL GAS TANK ★ MEAL PREP ★

DATE :

CLEANING CHEEKLIST

KEEP A GOOD THING GOING

EVERYDAY

	S	M	T	W	T	F	S
ONE LOAD OF LAUNDRY	◆	◆	◆	◆	◆	◆	◆
DISHES	◆	◆	◆	◆	◆	◆	◆
MAKE BEDS	◆	◆	◆	◆	◆	◆	◆
SPARY COUNTERTOPS	◆	◆	◆	◆	◆	◆	◆
PICK UP CLUTTER	◆	◆	◆	◆	◆	◆	◆
TRASH	◆	◆	◆	◆	◆	◆	◆
SORT MAIL	◆	◆	◆	◆	◆	◆	◆

MONTHLY

- DUST CEILING FANS
- CLEAN OVEN
- CLEAN INSIDE OF FRIDGE
- WASH WINDOWS
- PICK UP GARAGE
- PICK UP BASEMENT
- DUST/CLEAN BASEBOARDS
- GET RID OF ITEMS NO LONGER NEED
- ------------------------------
- ------------------------------
- ------------------------------
- ------------------------------

MON	KITCHEN	☆ CLEAN KITCHEN TABLE
		☆ WIPE DOWN SINK AND COUNTERS
		☆ VACUUM OR MOP
		☆ WIPE DOWN APPLIANCES
		☆

TUES	LIVINGROOM	☆ PICK UP CLUTTER
		☆ VACUUM OR MOP
		☆ WASH BLANKETS
		☆ DUST SURFACES
		☆

WED	BEDROOM	☆ PUT AWAY CLOTHES/PICK UP CLUTTER
		☆ DUST SURFACES
		☆ WASH BEDDING
		☆ VACUUM OR MOP
		☆

THUR	BATHROOM	☆ SANITIZE TOILET
		☆ VACUUM OR MOP
		☆ WASH SHOWER,SINK AND MIRRORS
		☆ WASH TOWELS AND MATS
		☆

FRI	DINING	☆ CLEAN OFF TABLE
		☆ VACUUM OR MOP
		☆ DUST SURFACES
		☆ PICK UP CLUTTER
		☆

SAT	ENTRY	☆ SANTIZE DOORKNOBS
		☆ DUST SURFACES
		☆ VACUUM OR MOP
		☆ PUT AWAY SHOES/COATS/HATS
		☆

SUN	GROCERY	☆ CLEAN OUT FRIDGE
		☆ MEAL PLAN
		☆ GROCERY SHOP AND FILL GAS TANK
		☆ MEAL PREP
		☆

DATE :

CLEANING CHEEKLIST

KEEP A GOOD THING GOING

EVERYDAY

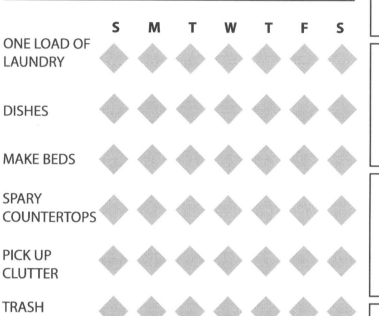

	S	M	T	W	T	F	S
ONE LOAD OF LAUNDRY	◆	◆	◆	◆	◆	◆	◆
DISHES	◆	◆	◆	◆	◆	◆	◆
MAKE BEDS	◆	◆	◆	◆	◆	◆	◆
SPARY COUNTERTOPS	◆	◆	◆	◆	◆	◆	◆
PICK UP CLUTTER	◆	◆	◆	◆	◆	◆	◆
TRASH	◆	◆	◆	◆	◆	◆	◆
SORT MAIL	◆	◆	◆	◆	◆	◆	◆

MONTHLY

- ⬡ DUST CEILING FANS
- ⬡ CLEAN OVEN
- ⬡ CLEAN INSIDE OF FRIDGE
- ⬡ WASH WINDOWS
- ⬡ PICK UP GARAGE
- ⬡ PICK UP BASEMENT
- ⬡ DUST/CLEAN BASEBOARDS
- ⬡ GET RID OF ITEMS NO LONGER NEED
- ⬡ ---------------------------------
- ⬡ ---------------------------------
- ⬡ ---------------------------------
- ⬡

MON — KITCHEN
- ★ CLEAN KITCHEN TABLE
- ★ WIPE DOWN SINK AND COUNTERS
- ★ VACUUM OR MOP
- ★ WIPE DOWN APPLIANCES
- ★

TUES — LIVING ROOM
- ★ PICK UP CLUTTER
- ★ VACUUM OR MOP
- ★ WASH BLANKETS
- ★ DUST SURFACES
- ★

WED — BEDROOM
- ★ PUT AWAY CLOTHES/PICK UP CLUTTER
- ★ DUST SURFACES
- ★ WASH BEDDING
- ★ VACUUM OR MOP
- ★

THUR — BATHROOM
- ★ SANITIZE TOILET
- ★ VACUUM OR MOP
- ★ WASH SHOWER,SINK AND MIRRORS
- ★ WASH TOWELS AND MATS
- ★

FRI — DINING
- ★ CLEAN OFF TABLE
- ★ VACUUM OR MOP
- ★ DUST SURFACES
- ★ PICK UP CLUTTER
- ★

SAT — ENTRY
- ★ SANTIZE DOORKNOBS
- ★ DUST SURFACES
- ★ VACUUM OR MOP
- ★ PUT AWAY SHOES/COATS/HATS
- ★

SUN — GROCERY
- ★ CLEAN OUT FRIDGE
- ★ MEAL PLAN
- ★ GROCERY SHOP AND FILL GAS TANK
- ★ MEAL PREP
- ★

CLEANING CHEEKLIST

KEEP A GOOD THING GOING

EVERYDAY

	S	M	T	W	T	F	S
ONE LOAD OF LAUNDRY	◆	◆	◆	◆	◆	◆	◆
DISHES	◆	◆	◆	◆	◆	◆	◆
MAKE BEDS	◆	◆	◆	◆	◆	◆	◆
SPARY COUNTERTOPS	◆	◆	◆	◆	◆	◆	◆
PICK UP CLUTTER	◆	◆	◆	◆	◆	◆	◆
TRASH	◆	◆	◆	◆	◆	◆	◆
SORT MAIL	◆	◆	◆	◆	◆	◆	◆

MONTHLY

- DUST CEILING FANS
- CLEAN OVEN
- CLEAN INSIDE OF FRIDGE
- WASH WINDOWS
- PICK UP GARAGE
- PICK UP BASEMENT
- DUST/CLEAN BASEBOARDS
- GET RID OF ITEMS NO LONGER NEED
- ------------------------------
- ------------------------------
- ------------------------------
- ------------------------------

MON — KITCHEN
- ★ CLEAN KITCHEN TABLE
- ★ WIPE DOWN SINK AND COUNTERS
- ★ VACUUM OR MOP
- ★ WIPE DOWN APPLIANCES
- ★

TUES — LIVING ROOM
- ★ PICK UP CLUTTER
- ★ VACUUM OR MOP
- ★ WASH BLANKETS
- ★ DUST SURFACES
- ★

WED — BEDROOM
- ★ PUT AWAY CLOTHES/PICK UP CLUTTER
- ★ DUST SURFACES
- ★ WASH BEDDING
- ★ VACUUM OR MOP
- ★

THUR — BATHROOM
- ★ SANITIZE TOILET
- ★ VACUUM OR MOP
- ★ WASH SHOWER, SINK AND MIRRORS
- ★ WASH TOWELS AND MATS
- ★

FRI — DINING
- ★ CLEAN OFF TABLE
- ★ VACUUM OR MOP
- ★ DUST SURFACES
- ★ PICK UP CLUTTER
- ★

SAT — ENTRY
- ★ SANTIZE DOORKNOBS
- ★ DUST SURFACES
- ★ VACUUM OR MOP
- ★ PUT AWAY SHOES/COATS/HATS
- ★

SUN — GROCERY
- ★ CLEAN OUT FRIDGE
- ★ MEAL PLAN
- ★ GROCERY SHOP AND FILL GAS TANK
- ★ MEAL PREP
- ★

DATE :

CLEANING CHEEKLIST

KEEP A GOOD THING GOING

EVERYDAY

	S	M	T	W	T	F	S
ONE LOAD OF LAUNDRY	◆	◆	◆	◆	◆	◆	◆
DISHES	◆	◆	◆	◆	◆	◆	◆
MAKE BEDS	◆	◆	◆	◆	◆	◆	◆
SPARY COUNTERTOPS	◆	◆	◆	◆	◆	◆	◆
PICK UP CLUTTER	◆	◆	◆	◆	◆	◆	◆
TRASH	◆	◆	◆	◆	◆	◆	◆
SORT MAIL	◆	◆	◆	◆	◆	◆	◆

MONTHLY

- DUST CEILING FANS
- CLEAN OVEN
- CLEAN INSIDE OF FRIDGE
- WASH WINDOWS
- PICK UP GARAGE
- PICK UP BASEMENT
- DUST/CLEAN BASEBOARDS
- GET RID OF ITEMS NO LONGER NEED
- _____
- _____
- _____
- _____

MON — KITCHEN
- ★ CLEAN KITCHEN TABLE
- ★ WIPE DOWN SINK AND COUNTERS
- ★ VACUUM OR MOP
- ★ WIPE DOWN APPLIANCES
- ★

TUES — LIVINGROOM
- ★ PICK UP CLUTTER
- ★ VACUUM OR MOP
- ★ WASH BLANKETS
- ★ DUST SURFACES
- ★

WED — BEDROOM
- ★ PUT AWAY CLOTHES/PICK UP CLUTTER
- ★ DUST SURFACES
- ★ WASH BEDDING
- ★ VACUUM OR MOP
- ★

THUR — BATHROOM
- ★ SANITIZE TOILET
- ★ VACUUM OR MOP
- ★ WASH SHOWER,SINK AND MIRRORS
- ★ WASH TOWELS AND MATS
- ★

FRI — DINING
- ★ CLEAN OFF TABLE
- ★ VACUUM OR MOP
- ★ DUST SURFACES
- ★ PICK UP CLUTTER
- ★

SAT — ENTRY
- ★ SANTIZE DOORKNOBS
- ★ DUST SURFACES
- ★ VACUUM OR MOP
- ★ PUT AWAY SHOES/COATS/HATS
- ★

SUN — GROCERY
- ★ CLEAN OUT FRIDGE
- ★ MEAL PLAN
- ★ GROCERY SHOP AND FILL GAS TANK
- ★ MEAL PREP
- ★

DATE :   # CLEANING CHEEKLIST

KEEP A GOOD THING GOING

EVERYDAY

	S	M	T	W	T	F	S
ONE LOAD OF LAUNDRY	◆	◆	◆	◆	◆	◆	◆
DISHES	◆	◆	◆	◆	◆	◆	◆
MAKE BEDS	◆	◆	◆	◆	◆	◆	◆
SPARY COUNTERTOPS	◆	◆	◆	◆	◆	◆	◆
PICK UP CLUTTER	◆	◆	◆	◆	◆	◆	◆
TRASH	◆	◆	◆	◆	◆	◆	◆
SORT MAIL	◆	◆	◆	◆	◆	◆	◆

MONTHLY

- DUST CEILING FANS
- CLEAN OVEN
- CLEAN INSIDE OF FRIDGE
- WASH WINDOWS
- PICK UP GARAGE
- PICK UP BASEMENT
- DUST/CLEAN BASEBOARDS
- GET RID OF ITEMS NO LONGER NEED
- ------------------------------
- ------------------------------
- ------------------------------
- ------------------------------

MON	KITCHEN	☆ CLEAN KITCHEN TABLE ☆ WIPE DOWN SINK AND COUNTERS ☆ VACUUM OR MOP ☆ WIPE DOWN APPLIANCES ☆
TUES	LIVINGROOM	☆ PICK UP CLUTTER ☆ VACUUM OR MOP ☆ WASH BLANKETS ☆ DUST SURFACES ☆
WED	BEDROOM	☆ PUT AWAY CLOTHES/PICK UP CLUTTER ☆ DUST SURFACES ☆ WASH BEDDING ☆ VACUUM OR MOP ☆
THUR	BATHROOM	☆ SANITIZE TOILET ☆ VACUUM OR MOP ☆ WASH SHOWER,SINK AND MIRRORS ☆ WASH TOWELS AND MATS ☆
FRI	DINING	☆ CLEAN OFF TABLE ☆ VACUUM OR MOP ☆ DUST SURFACES ☆ PICK UP CLUTTER ☆
SAT	ENTRY	☆ SANTIZE DOORKNOBS ☆ DUST SURFACES ☆ VACUUM OR MOP ☆ PUT AWAY SHOES/COATS/HATS ☆
SUN	GROCERY	☆ CLEAN OUT FRIDGE ☆ MEAL PLAN ☆ GROCERY SHOP AND FILL GAS TANK ☆ MEAL PREP ☆

CLEANING CHEEKLIST

DATE :

KEEP A GOOD THING GOING

EVERYDAY

	S	M	T	W	T	F	S
ONE LOAD OF LAUNDRY	◆	◆	◆	◆	◆	◆	◆
DISHES	◆	◆	◆	◆	◆	◆	◆
MAKE BEDS	◆	◆	◆	◆	◆	◆	◆
SPARY COUNTERTOPS	◆	◆	◆	◆	◆	◆	◆
PICK UP CLUTTER	◆	◆	◆	◆	◆	◆	◆
TRASH	◆	◆	◆	◆	◆	◆	◆
SORT MAIL	◆	◆	◆	◆	◆	◆	◆

MONTHLY

- DUST CEILING FANS
- CLEAN OVEN
- CLEAN INSIDE OF FRIDGE
- WASH WINDOWS
- PICK UP GARAGE
- PICK UP BASEMENT
- DUST/CLEAN BASEBOARDS
- GET RID OF ITEMS NO LONGER NEED
- -
- -
- -

MON — KITCHEN
- ★ CLEAN KITCHEN TABLE
- ★ WIPE DOWN SINK AND COUNTERS
- ★ VACUUM OR MOP
- ★ WIPE DOWN APPLIANCES
- ★

TUES — LIVINGROOM
- ★ PICK UP CLUTTER
- ★ VACUUM OR MOP
- ★ WASH BLANKETS
- ★ DUST SURFACES
- ★

WED — BEDROOM
- ★ PUT AWAY CLOTHES/PICK UP CLUTTER
- ★ DUST SURFACES
- ★ WASH BEDDING
- ★ VACUUM OR MOP
- ★

THUR — BATHROOM
- ★ SANITIZE TOILET
- ★ VACUUM OR MOP
- ★ WASH SHOWER,SINK AND MIRRORS
- ★ WASH TOWELS AND MATS
- ★

FRI — DINING
- ★ CLEAN OFF TABLE
- ★ VACUUM OR MOP
- ★ DUST SURFACES
- ★ PICK UP CLUTTER

SAT — ENTRY
- ★ SANTIZE DOORKNOBS
- ★ DUST SURFACES
- ★ VACUUM OR MOP
- ★ PUT AWAY SHOES/COATS/HATS
- ★

SUN — GROCERY
- ★ CLEAN OUT FRIDGE
- ★ MEAL PLAN
- ★ GROCERY SHOP AND FILL GAS TANK
- ★ MEAL PREP
- ★

DATE :

CLEANING CHEEKLIST

KEEP A GOOD THING GOING

EVERYDAY

	S	M	T	W	T	F	S
ONE LOAD OF LAUNDRY	◆	◆	◆	◆	◆	◆	◆
DISHES	◆	◆	◆	◆	◆	◆	◆
MAKE BEDS	◆	◆	◆	◆	◆	◆	◆
SPARY COUNTERTOPS	◆	◆	◆	◆	◆	◆	◆
PICK UP CLUTTER	◆	◆	◆	◆	◆	◆	◆
TRASH	◆	◆	◆	◆	◆	◆	◆
SORT MAIL	◆	◆	◆	◆	◆	◆	◆

MONTHLY

- DUST CEILING FANS
- CLEAN OVEN
- CLEAN INSIDE OF FRIDGE
- WASH WINDOWS
- PICK UP GARAGE
- PICK UP BASEMENT
- DUST/CLEAN BASEBOARDS
- GET RID OF ITEMS NO LONGER NEED
- ------------------------------
- ------------------------------
- ------------------------------
- ------------------------------

MON	KITCHEN	★ CLEAN KITCHEN TABLE ★ WIPE DOWN SINK AND COUNTERS ★ VACUUM OR MOP ★ WIPE DOWN APPLIANCES ★
TUES	LIVING ROOM	★ PICK UP CLUTTER ★ VACUUM OR MOP ★ WASH BLANKETS ★ DUST SURFACES ★
WED	BEDROOM	★ PUT AWAY CLOTHES/PICK UP CLUTTER ★ DUST SURFACES ★ WASH BEDDING ★ VACUUM OR MOP ★
THUR	BATHROOM	★ SANITIZE TOILET ★ VACUUM OR MOP ★ WASH SHOWER,SINK AND MIRRORS ★ WASH TOWELS AND MATS ★
FRI	DINING	★ CLEAN OFF TABLE ★ VACUUM OR MOP ★ DUST SURFACES ★ PICK UP CLUTTER ★
SAT	ENTRY	★ SANTIZE DOORKNOBS ★ DUST SURFACES ★ VACUUM OR MOP ★ PUT AWAY SHOES/COATS/HATS ★
SUN	GROCERY	★ CLEAN OUT FRIDGE ★ MEAL PLAN ★ GROCERY SHOP AND FILL GAS TANK ★ MEAL PREP ★

DATE :

CLEANING CHEEKLIST

KEEP A GOOD THING GOING

EVERYDAY

	S	M	T	W	T	F	S
ONE LOAD OF LAUNDRY	◆	◆	◆	◆	◆	◆	◆
DISHES	◆	◆	◆	◆	◆	◆	◆
MAKE BEDS	◆	◆	◆	◆	◆	◆	◆
SPARY COUNTERTOPS	◆	◆	◆	◆	◆	◆	◆
PICK UP CLUTTER	◆	◆	◆	◆	◆	◆	◆
TRASH	◆	◆	◆	◆	◆	◆	◆
SORT MAIL	◆	◆	◆	◆	◆	◆	◆

MONTHLY

- ⬡ DUST CEILING FANS
- ⬡ CLEAN OVEN
- ⬡ CLEAN INSIDE OF FRIDGE
- ⬡ WASH WINDOWS
- ⬡ PICK UP GARAGE
- ⬡ PICK UP BASEMENT
- ⬡ DUST/CLEAN BASEBOARDS
- ⬡ GET RID OF ITEMS NO LONGER NEED
- ⬡ ----------------------------------
- ⬡ ----------------------------------
- ⬡ ----------------------------------
- ⬡ ----------------------------------

MON — KITCHEN
- ★ CLEAN KITCHEN TABLE
- ★ WIPE DOWN SINK AND COUNTERS
- ★ VACUUM OR MOP
- ★ WIPE DOWN APPLIANCES
- ★

TUES — LIVINGROOM
- ★ PICK UP CLUTTER
- ★ VACUUM OR MOP
- ★ WASH BLANKETS
- ★ DUST SURFACES
- ★

WED — BEDROOM
- ★ PUT AWAY CLOTHES/PICK UP CLUTTER
- ★ DUST SURFACES
- ★ WASH BEDDING
- ★ VACUUM OR MOP
- ★

THUR — BATHROOM
- ★ SANITIZE TOILET
- ★ VACUUM OR MOP
- ★ WASH SHOWER,SINK AND MIRRORS
- ★ WASH TOWELS AND MATS
- ★

FRI — DINING
- ★ CLEAN OFF TABLE
- ★ VACUUM OR MOP
- ★ DUST SURFACES
- ★ PICK UP CLUTTER
- ★

SAT — ENTRY
- ★ SANTIZE DOORKNOBS
- ★ DUST SURFACES
- ★ VACUUM OR MOP
- ★ PUT AWAY SHOES/COATS/HATS
- ★

SUN — GROCERY
- ★ CLEAN OUT FRIDGE
- ★ MEAL PLAN
- ★ GROCERY SHOP AND FILL GAS TANK
- ★ MEAL PREP
- ★

DATE :

CLEANING CHEEKLIST

KEEP A GOOD THING GOING

EVERYDAY

	S	M	T	W	T	F	S
ONE LOAD OF LAUNDRY	◆	◆	◆	◆	◆	◆	◆
DISHES	◆	◆	◆	◆	◆	◆	◆
MAKE BEDS	◆	◆	◆	◆	◆	◆	◆
SPARY COUNTERTOPS	◆	◆	◆	◆	◆	◆	◆
PICK UP CLUTTER	◆	◆	◆	◆	◆	◆	◆
TRASH	◆	◆	◆	◆	◆	◆	◆
SORT MAIL	◆	◆	◆	◆	◆	◆	◆

MONTHLY

- DUST CEILING FANS
- CLEAN OVEN
- CLEAN INSIDE OF FRIDGE
- WASH WINDOWS
- PICK UP GARAGE
- PICK UP BASEMENT
- DUST/CLEAN BASEBOARDS
- GET RID OF ITEMS NO LONGER NEED
- - - - - - - - - - - - - - - - - - - -
- - - - - - - - - - - - - - - - - - - -
- - - - - - - - - - - - - - - - - - - -
- - - - - - - - - - - - - - - - - - - -

MON	KITCHEN	★ CLEAN KITCHEN TABLE ★ WIPE DOWN SINK AND COUNTERS ★ VACUUM OR MOP ★ WIPE DOWN APPLIANCES ★
TUES	LIVINGROOM	★ PICK UP CLUTTER ★ VACUUM OR MOP ★ WASH BLANKETS ★ DUST SURFACES ★
WED	BEDROOM	★ PUT AWAY CLOTHES/PICK UP CLUTTER ★ DUST SURFACES ★ WASH BEDDING ★ VACUUM OR MOP ★
THUR	BATHROOM	★ SANITIZE TOILET ★ VACUUM OR MOP ★ WASH SHOWER,SINK AND MIRRORS ★ WASH TOWELS AND MATS ★
FRI	DINING	★ CLEAN OFF TABLE ★ VACUUM OR MOP ★ DUST SURFACES ★ PICK UP CLUTTER ★
SAT	ENTRY	★ SANTIZE DOORKNOBS ★ DUST SURFACES ★ VACUUM OR MOP ★ PUT AWAY SHOES/COATS/HATS ★
SUN	GROCERY	★ CLEAN OUT FRIDGE ★ MEAL PLAN ★ GROCERY SHOP AND FILL GAS TANK ★ MEAL PREP ★

DATE:

CLEANING CHECKLIST

KEEP A GOOD THING GOING

EVERYDAY

	S	M	T	W	T	F	S
ONE LOAD OF LAUNDRY	◆	◆	◆	◆	◆	◆	◆
DISHES	◆	◆	◆	◆	◆	◆	◆
MAKE BEDS	◆	◆	◆	◆	◆	◆	◆
SPARY COUNTERTOPS	◆	◆	◆	◆	◆	◆	◆
PICK UP CLUTTER	◆	◆	◆	◆	◆	◆	◆
TRASH	◆	◆	◆	◆	◆	◆	◆
SORT MAIL	◆	◆	◆	◆	◆	◆	◆

MONTHLY

- DUST CEILING FANS
- CLEAN OVEN
- CLEAN INSIDE OF FRIDGE
- WASH WINDOWS
- PICK UP GARAGE
- PICK UP BASEMENT
- DUST/CLEAN BASEBOARDS
- GET RID OF ITEMS NO LONGER NEED
- -
- -
- -
- -

MON — KITCHEN
- ★ CLEAN KITCHEN TABLE
- ★ WIPE DOWN SINK AND COUNTERS
- ★ VACUUM OR MOP
- ★ WIPE DOWN APPLIANCES
- ★

TUES — LIVING ROOM
- ★ PICK UP CLUTTER
- ★ VACUUM OR MOP
- ★ WASH BLANKETS
- ★ DUST SURFACES
- ★

WED — BEDROOM
- ★ PUT AWAY CLOTHES/PICK UP CLUTTER
- ★ DUST SURFACES
- ★ WASH BEDDING
- ★ VACUUM OR MOP
- ★

THUR — BATHROOM
- ★ SANITIZE TOILET
- ★ VACUUM OR MOP
- ★ WASH SHOWER,SINK AND MIRRORS
- ★ WASH TOWELS AND MATS
- ★

FRI — DINING
- ★ CLEAN OFF TABLE
- ★ VACUUM OR MOP
- ★ DUST SURFACES
- ★ PICK UP CLUTTER

SAT — ENTRY
- ★ SANTIZE DOORKNOBS
- ★ DUST SURFACES
- ★ VACUUM OR MOP
- ★ PUT AWAY SHOES/COATS/HATS
- ★

SUN — GROCERY
- ★ CLEAN OUT FRIDGE
- ★ MEAL PLAN
- ★ GROCERY SHOP AND FILL GAS TANK
- ★ MEAL PREP

DATE :

CLEANING CHEEKLIST

KEEP A GOOD THING GOING

EVERYDAY

	S	M	T	W	T	F	S
ONE LOAD OF LAUNDRY	◆	◆	◆	◆	◆	◆	◆
DISHES	◆	◆	◆	◆	◆	◆	◆
MAKE BEDS	◆	◆	◆	◆	◆	◆	◆
SPARY COUNTERTOPS	◆	◆	◆	◆	◆	◆	◆
PICK UP CLUTTER	◆	◆	◆	◆	◆	◆	◆
TRASH	◆	◆	◆	◆	◆	◆	◆
SORT MAIL	◆	◆	◆	◆	◆	◆	◆

MONTHLY

- DUST CEILING FANS
- CLEAN OVEN
- CLEAN INSIDE OF FRIDGE
- WASH WINDOWS
- PICK UP GARAGE
- PICK UP BASEMENT
- DUST/CLEAN BASEBOARDS
- GET RID OF ITEMS NO LONGER NEED
- -
- -
- -
- -

MON — KITCHEN
- ★ CLEAN KITCHEN TABLE
- ★ WIPE DOWN SINK AND COUNTERS
- ★ VACUUM OR MOP
- ★ WIPE DOWN APPLIANCES
- ★

TUES — LIVING ROOM
- ★ PICK UP CLUTTER
- ★ VACUUM OR MOP
- ★ WASH BLANKETS
- ★ DUST SURFACES
- ★

WED — BEDROOM
- ★ PUT AWAY CLOTHES/PICK UP CLUTTER
- ★ DUST SURFACES
- ★ WASH BEDDING
- ★ VACUUM OR MOP
- ★

THUR — BATHROOM
- ★ SANITIZE TOILET
- ★ VACUUM OR MOP
- ★ WASH SHOWER,SINK AND MIRRORS
- ★ WASH TOWELS AND MATS
- ★

FRI — DINING
- ★ CLEAN OFF TABLE
- ★ VACUUM OR MOP
- ★ DUST SURFACES
- ★ PICK UP CLUTTER
- ★

SAT — ENTRY
- ★ SANTIZE DOORKNOBS
- ★ DUST SURFACES
- ★ VACUUM OR MOP
- ★ PUT AWAY SHOES/COATS/HATS
- ★

SUN — GROCERY
- ★ CLEAN OUT FRIDGE
- ★ MEAL PLAN
- ★ GROCERY SHOP AND FILL GAS TANK
- ★ MEAL PREP
- ★

DATE :

CLEANING CHEEKLIST

KEEP A GOOD THING GOING

EVERYDAY

	S	M	T	W	T	F	S
ONE LOAD OF LAUNDRY	◆	◆	◆	◆	◆	◆	◆
DISHES	◆	◆	◆	◆	◆	◆	◆
MAKE BEDS	◆	◆	◆	◆	◆	◆	◆
SPARY COUNTERTOPS	◆	◆	◆	◆	◆	◆	◆
PICK UP CLUTTER	◆	◆	◆	◆	◆	◆	◆
TRASH	◆	◆	◆	◆	◆	◆	◆
SORT MAIL	◆	◆	◆	◆	◆	◆	◆

MONTHLY

- ⬡ DUST CEILING FANS
- ⬡ CLEAN OVEN
- ⬡ CLEAN INSIDE OF FRIDGE
- ⬡ WASH WINDOWS
- ⬡ PICK UP GARAGE
- ⬡ PICK UP BASEMENT
- ⬡ DUST/CLEAN BASEBOARDS
- ⬡ GET RID OF ITEMS NO LONGER NEED
- ⬡ _____
- ⬡ _____
- ⬡ _____
- ⬡ _____

MON — KITCHEN
- ☆ CLEAN KITCHEN TABLE
- ☆ WIPE DOWN SINK AND COUNTERS
- ☆ VACUUM OR MOP
- ☆ WIPE DOWN APPLIANCES
- ☆

TUES — LIVING ROOM
- ☆ PICK UP CLUTTER
- ☆ VACUUM OR MOP
- ☆ WASH BLANKETS
- ☆ DUST SURFACES
- ☆

WED — BEDROOM
- ☆ PUT AWAY CLOTHES/PICK UP CLUTTER
- ☆ DUST SURFACES
- ☆ WASH BEDDING
- ☆ VACUUM OR MOP
- ☆

THUR — BATHROOM
- ☆ SANITIZE TOILET
- ☆ VACUUM OR MOP
- ☆ WASH SHOWER,SINK AND MIRRORS
- ☆ WASH TOWELS AND MATS
- ☆

FRI — DINING
- ☆ CLEAN OFF TABLE
- ☆ VACUUM OR MOP
- ☆ DUST SURFACES
- ☆ PICK UP CLUTTER
- ☆

SAT — ENTRY
- ☆ SANTIZE DOORKNOBS
- ☆ DUST SURFACES
- ☆ VACUUM OR MOP
- ☆ PUT AWAY SHOES/COATS/HATS
- ☆

SUN — GROCERY
- ☆ CLEAN OUT FRIDGE
- ☆ MEAL PLAN
- ☆ GROCERY SHOP AND FILL GAS TANK
- ☆ MEAL PREP
- ☆

DATE :

CLEANING CHEEKLIST

KEEP A GOOD THING GOING

EVERYDAY

	S	M	T	W	T	F	S
ONE LOAD OF LAUNDRY	◆	◆	◆	◆	◆	◆	◆
DISHES	◆	◆	◆	◆	◆	◆	◆
MAKE BEDS	◆	◆	◆	◆	◆	◆	◆
SPARY COUNTERTOPS	◆	◆	◆	◆	◆	◆	◆
PICK UP CLUTTER	◆	◆	◆	◆	◆	◆	◆
TRASH	◆	◆	◆	◆	◆	◆	◆
SORT MAIL	◆	◆	◆	◆	◆	◆	◆

MONTHLY

- DUST CEILING FANS
- CLEAN OVEN
- CLEAN INSIDE OF FRIDGE
- WASH WINDOWS
- PICK UP GARAGE
- PICK UP BASEMENT
- DUST/CLEAN BASEBOARDS
- GET RID OF ITEMS NO LONGER NEED
- _____
- _____
- _____
- _____

MON — KITCHEN
- ★ CLEAN KITCHEN TABLE
- ★ WIPE DOWN SINK AND COUNTERS
- ★ VACUUM OR MOP
- ★ WIPE DOWN APPLIANCES
- ★

TUES — LIVINGROOM
- ★ PICK UP CLUTTER
- ★ VACUUM OR MOP
- ★ WASH BLANKETS
- ★ DUST SURFACES
- ★

WED — BEDROOM
- ★ PUT AWAY CLOTHES/PICK UP CLUTTER
- ★ DUST SURFACES
- ★ WASH BEDDING
- ★ VACUUM OR MOP
- ★

THUR — BATHROOM
- ★ SANITIZE TOILET
- ★ VACUUM OR MOP
- ★ WASH SHOWER,SINK AND MIRRORS
- ★ WASH TOWELS AND MATS
- ★

FRI — DINING
- ★ CLEAN OFF TABLE
- ★ VACUUM OR MOP
- ★ DUST SURFACES
- ★ PICK UP CLUTTER
- ★

SAT — ENTRY
- ★ SANTIZE DOORKNOBS
- ★ DUST SURFACES
- ★ VACUUM OR MOP
- ★ PUT AWAY SHOES/COATS/HATS
- ★

SUN — GROCERY
- ★ CLEAN OUT FRIDGE
- ★ MEAL PLAN
- ★ GROCERY SHOP AND FILL GAS TANK
- ★ MEAL PREP
- ★

CLEANING CHEEKLIST

KEEP A GOOD THING GOING

EVERYDAY

	S	M	T	W	T	F	S
ONE LOAD OF LAUNDRY	◆	◆	◆	◆	◆	◆	◆
DISHES	◆	◆	◆	◆	◆	◆	◆
MAKE BEDS	◆	◆	◆	◆	◆	◆	◆
SPARY COUNTERTOPS	◆	◆	◆	◆	◆	◆	◆
PICK UP CLUTTER	◆	◆	◆	◆	◆	◆	◆
TRASH	◆	◆	◆	◆	◆	◆	◆
SORT MAIL	◆	◆	◆	◆	◆	◆	◆

MONTHLY

- DUST CEILING FANS
- CLEAN OVEN
- CLEAN INSIDE OF FRIDGE
- WASH WINDOWS
- PICK UP GARAGE
- PICK UP BASEMENT
- DUST/CLEAN BASEBOARDS
- GET RID OF ITEMS NO LONGER NEED
- ----------------------------
- ----------------------------
- ----------------------------
-

MON — KITCHEN
- ★ CLEAN KITCHEN TABLE
- ★ WIPE DOWN SINK AND COUNTERS
- ★ VACUUM OR MOP
- ★ WIPE DOWN APPLIANCES
- ★

TUES — LIVINGROOM
- ★ PICK UP CLUTTER
- ★ VACUUM OR MOP
- ★ WASH BLANKETS
- ★ DUST SURFACES
- ★

WED — BEDROOM
- ★ PUT AWAY CLOTHES/PICK UP CLUTTER
- ★ DUST SURFACES
- ★ WASH BEDDING
- ★ VACUUM OR MOP
- ★

THUR — BATHROOM
- ★ SANITIZE TOILET
- ★ VACUUM OR MOP
- ★ WASH SHOWER,SINK AND MIRRORS
- ★ WASH TOWELS AND MATS
- ★

FRI — DINING
- ★ CLEAN OFF TABLE
- ★ VACUUM OR MOP
- ★ DUST SURFACES
- ★ PICK UP CLUTTER
- ★

SAT — ENTRY
- ★ SANTIZE DOORKNOBS
- ★ DUST SURFACES
- ★ VACUUM OR MOP
- ★ PUT AWAY SHOES/COATS/HATS
- ★

SUN — GROCERY
- ★ CLEAN OUT FRIDGE
- ★ MEAL PLAN
- ★ GROCERY SHOP AND FILL GAS TANK
- ★ MEAL PREP
- ★

DATE :

CLEANING CHEEKLIST

KEEP A GOOD THING GOING

EVERYDAY

	S	M	T	W	T	F	S
ONE LOAD OF LAUNDRY	◆	◆	◆	◆	◆	◆	◆
DISHES	◆	◆	◆	◆	◆	◆	◆
MAKE BEDS	◆	◆	◆	◆	◆	◆	◆
SPARY COUNTERTOPS	◆	◆	◆	◆	◆	◆	◆
PICK UP CLUTTER	◆	◆	◆	◆	◆	◆	◆
TRASH	◆	◆	◆	◆	◆	◆	◆
SORT MAIL	◆	◆	◆	◆	◆	◆	◆

MONTHLY

- ⬡ DUST CEILING FANS
- ⬡ CLEAN OVEN
- ⬡ CLEAN INSIDE OF FRIDGE
- ⬡ WASH WINDOWS
- ⬡ PICK UP GARAGE
- ⬡ PICK UP BASEMENT
- ⬡ DUST/CLEAN BASEBOARDS
- ⬡ GET RID OF ITEMS NO LONGER NEED
- ⬡ -
- ⬡ -
- ⬡ -
- ⬡ -

MON	KITCHEN	★ CLEAN KITCHEN TABLE ★ WIPE DOWN SINK AND COUNTERS ★ VACUUM OR MOP ★ WIPE DOWN APPLIANCES ★
TUES	LIVINGROOM	★ PICK UP CLUTTER ★ VACUUM OR MOP ★ WASH BLANKETS ★ DUST SURFACES ★
WED	BEDROOM	★ PUT AWAY CLOTHES/PICK UP CLUTTER ★ DUST SURFACES ★ WASH BEDDING ★ VACUUM OR MOP ★
THUR	BATHROOM	★ SANITIZE TOILET ★ VACUUM OR MOP ★ WASH SHOWER,SINK AND MIRRORS ★ WASH TOWELS AND MATS ★
FRI	DINING	★ CLEAN OFF TABLE ★ VACUUM OR MOP ★ DUST SURFACES ★ PICK UP CLUTTER ★
SAT	ENTRY	★ SANTIZE DOORKNOBS ★ DUST SURFACES ★ VACUUM OR MOP ★ PUT AWAY SHOES/COATS/HATS ★
SUN	GROCERY	★ CLEAN OUT FRIDGE ★ MEAL PLAN ★ GROCERY SHOP AND FILL GAS TANK ★ MEAL PREP ★

DATE :

CLEANING CHEEKLIST

KEEP A GOOD THING GOING

EVERYDAY

	S	M	T	W	T	F	S
ONE LOAD OF LAUNDRY	◆	◆	◆	◆	◆	◆	◆
DISHES	◆	◆	◆	◆	◆	◆	◆
MAKE BEDS	◆	◆	◆	◆	◆	◆	◆
SPARY COUNTERTOPS	◆	◆	◆	◆	◆	◆	◆
PICK UP CLUTTER	◆	◆	◆	◆	◆	◆	◆
TRASH	◆	◆	◆	◆	◆	◆	◆
SORT MAIL	◆	◆	◆	◆	◆	◆	◆

MONTHLY

- ⬡ DUST CEILING FANS
- ⬡ CLEAN OVEN
- ⬡ CLEAN INSIDE OF FRIDGE
- ⬡ WASH WINDOWS
- ⬡ PICK UP GARAGE
- ⬡ PICK UP BASEMENT
- ⬡ DUST/CLEAN BASEBOARDS
- ⬡ GET RID OF ITEMS NO LONGER NEED
- ⬡ ------------------------------
- ⬡ ------------------------------
- ⬡ ------------------------------
- ⬡

MON — KITCHEN
- ★ CLEAN KITCHEN TABLE
- ★ WIPE DOWN SINK AND COUNTERS
- ★ VACUUM OR MOP
- ★ WIPE DOWN APPLIANCES
- ★

TUES — LIVINGROOM
- ★ PICK UP CLUTTER
- ★ VACUUM OR MOP
- ★ WASH BLANKETS
- ★ DUST SURFACES
- ★

WED — BEDROOM
- ★ PUT AWAY CLOTHES/PICK UP CLUTTER
- ★ DUST SURFACES
- ★ WASH BEDDING
- ★ VACUUM OR MOP
- ★

THUR — BATHROOM
- ★ SANITIZE TOILET
- ★ VACUUM OR MOP
- ★ WASH SHOWER,SINK AND MIRRORS
- ★ WASH TOWELS AND MATS
- ★

FRI — DINING
- ★ CLEAN OFF TABLE
- ★ VACUUM OR MOP
- ★ DUST SURFACES
- ★ PICK UP CLUTTER

SAT — ENTRY
- ★ SANTIZE DOORKNOBS
- ★ DUST SURFACES
- ★ VACUUM OR MOP
- ★ PUT AWAY SHOES/COATS/HATS
- ★

SUN — GROCERY
- ★ CLEAN OUT FRIDGE
- ★ MEAL PLAN
- ★ GROCERY SHOP AND FILL GAS TANK
- ★ MEAL PREP
- ★

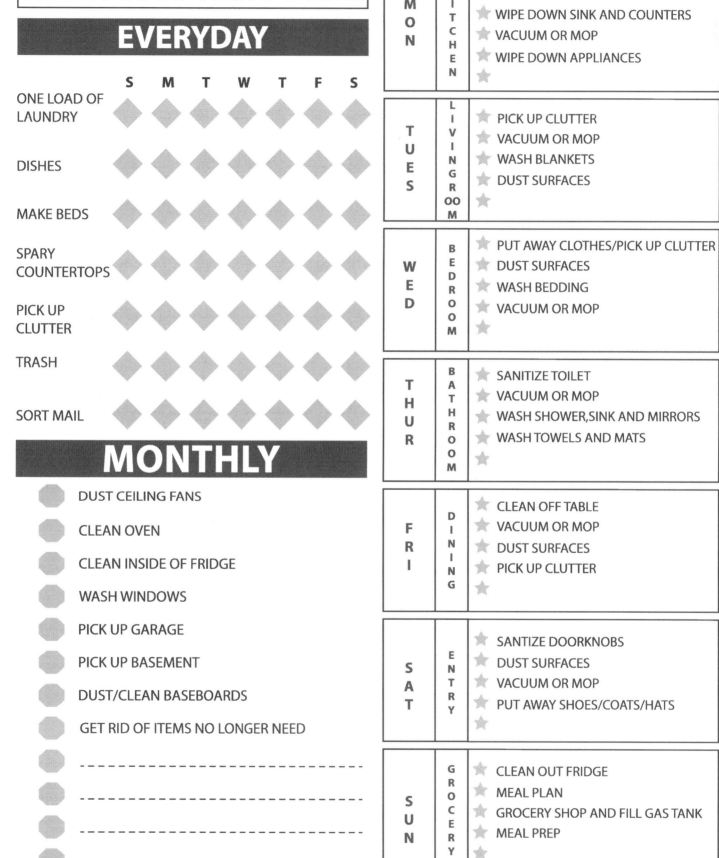

DATE :

CLEANING CHEEKLIST

KEEP A GOOD THING GOING

EVERYDAY

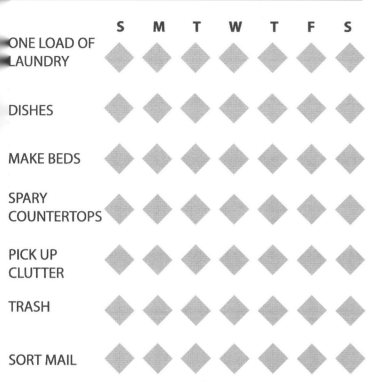

	S	M	T	W	T	F	S
ONE LOAD OF LAUNDRY	◆	◆	◆	◆	◆	◆	◆
DISHES	◆	◆	◆	◆	◆	◆	◆
MAKE BEDS	◆	◆	◆	◆	◆	◆	◆
SPARY COUNTERTOPS	◆	◆	◆	◆	◆	◆	◆
PICK UP CLUTTER	◆	◆	◆	◆	◆	◆	◆
TRASH	◆	◆	◆	◆	◆	◆	◆
SORT MAIL	◆	◆	◆	◆	◆	◆	◆

MONTHLY

- DUST CEILING FANS
- CLEAN OVEN
- CLEAN INSIDE OF FRIDGE
- WASH WINDOWS
- PICK UP GARAGE
- PICK UP BASEMENT
- DUST/CLEAN BASEBOARDS
- GET RID OF ITEMS NO LONGER NEED
- - - - - - - - - - - - - - - - -
- - - - - - - - - - - - - - - - -
- - - - - - - - - - - - - - - - -
- - - - - - - - - - - - - - - - -

MON	KITCHEN	☆ CLEAN KITCHEN TABLE
		☆ WIPE DOWN SINK AND COUNTERS
		☆ VACUUM OR MOP
		☆ WIPE DOWN APPLIANCES
		☆

TUES	LIVINGROOM	☆ PICK UP CLUTTER
		☆ VACUUM OR MOP
		☆ WASH BLANKETS
		☆ DUST SURFACES
		☆

WED	BEDROOM	☆ PUT AWAY CLOTHES/PICK UP CLUTTER
		☆ DUST SURFACES
		☆ WASH BEDDING
		☆ VACUUM OR MOP
		☆

THUR	BATHROOM	☆ SANITIZE TOILET
		☆ VACUUM OR MOP
		☆ WASH SHOWER,SINK AND MIRRORS
		☆ WASH TOWELS AND MATS
		☆

FRI	DINING	☆ CLEAN OFF TABLE
		☆ VACUUM OR MOP
		☆ DUST SURFACES
		☆ PICK UP CLUTTER
		☆

SAT	ENTRY	☆ SANTIZE DOORKNOBS
		☆ DUST SURFACES
		☆ VACUUM OR MOP
		☆ PUT AWAY SHOES/COATS/HATS
		☆

SUN	GROCERY	☆ CLEAN OUT FRIDGE
		☆ MEAL PLAN
		☆ GROCERY SHOP AND FILL GAS TANK
		☆ MEAL PREP
		☆

DATE :   # CLEANING CHEEKLIST

KEEP A GOOD THING GOING

EVERYDAY

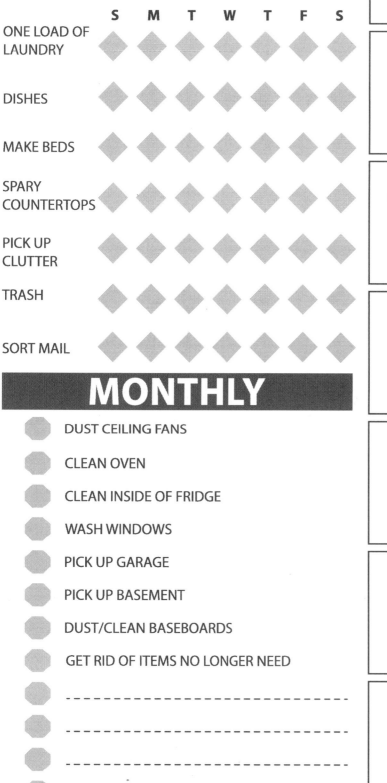

	S	M	T	W	T	F	S
ONE LOAD OF LAUNDRY	◆	◆	◆	◆	◆	◆	◆
DISHES	◆	◆	◆	◆	◆	◆	◆
MAKE BEDS	◆	◆	◆	◆	◆	◆	◆
SPARY COUNTERTOPS	◆	◆	◆	◆	◆	◆	◆
PICK UP CLUTTER	◆	◆	◆	◆	◆	◆	◆
TRASH	◆	◆	◆	◆	◆	◆	◆
SORT MAIL	◆	◆	◆	◆	◆	◆	◆

MONTHLY

- DUST CEILING FANS
- CLEAN OVEN
- CLEAN INSIDE OF FRIDGE
- WASH WINDOWS
- PICK UP GARAGE
- PICK UP BASEMENT
- DUST/CLEAN BASEBOARDS
- GET RID OF ITEMS NO LONGER NEED
- ----------------------------------
- ----------------------------------
- ----------------------------------
- ----------------------------------

MON — **KITCHEN**
- ★ CLEAN KITCHEN TABLE
- ★ WIPE DOWN SINK AND COUNTERS
- ★ VACUUM OR MOP
- ★ WIPE DOWN APPLIANCES
- ★

TUES — **LIVINGROOM**
- ★ PICK UP CLUTTER
- ★ VACUUM OR MOP
- ★ WASH BLANKETS
- ★ DUST SURFACES
- ★

WED — **BEDROOM**
- ★ PUT AWAY CLOTHES/PICK UP CLUTTER
- ★ DUST SURFACES
- ★ WASH BEDDING
- ★ VACUUM OR MOP
- ★

THUR — **BATHROOM**
- ★ SANITIZE TOILET
- ★ VACUUM OR MOP
- ★ WASH SHOWER,SINK AND MIRRORS
- ★ WASH TOWELS AND MATS
- ★

FRI — **DINING**
- ★ CLEAN OFF TABLE
- ★ VACUUM OR MOP
- ★ DUST SURFACES
- ★ PICK UP CLUTTER
- ★

SAT — **ENTRY**
- ★ SANTIZE DOORKNOBS
- ★ DUST SURFACES
- ★ VACUUM OR MOP
- ★ PUT AWAY SHOES/COATS/HATS
- ★

SUN — **GROCERY**
- ★ CLEAN OUT FRIDGE
- ★ MEAL PLAN
- ★ GROCERY SHOP AND FILL GAS TANK
- ★ MEAL PREP
- ★

DATE :

CLEANING CHEEKLIST

KEEP A GOOD THING GOING

EVERYDAY

	S	M	T	W	T	F	S
ONE LOAD OF LAUNDRY	◆	◆	◆	◆	◆	◆	◆
DISHES	◆	◆	◆	◆	◆	◆	◆
MAKE BEDS	◆	◆	◆	◆	◆	◆	◆
SPARY COUNTERTOPS	◆	◆	◆	◆	◆	◆	◆
PICK UP CLUTTER	◆	◆	◆	◆	◆	◆	◆
TRASH	◆	◆	◆	◆	◆	◆	◆
SORT MAIL	◆	◆	◆	◆	◆	◆	◆

MONTHLY

- DUST CEILING FANS
- CLEAN OVEN
- CLEAN INSIDE OF FRIDGE
- WASH WINDOWS
- PICK UP GARAGE
- PICK UP BASEMENT
- DUST/CLEAN BASEBOARDS
- GET RID OF ITEMS NO LONGER NEED
- -------------------------
- -------------------------
- -------------------------
- -------------------------

MON	KITCHEN	★ CLEAN KITCHEN TABLE ★ WIPE DOWN SINK AND COUNTERS ★ VACUUM OR MOP ★ WIPE DOWN APPLIANCES ★
TUES	LIVING ROOM	★ PICK UP CLUTTER ★ VACUUM OR MOP ★ WASH BLANKETS ★ DUST SURFACES ★
WED	BEDROOM	★ PUT AWAY CLOTHES/PICK UP CLUTTER ★ DUST SURFACES ★ WASH BEDDING ★ VACUUM OR MOP ★
THUR	BATHROOM	★ SANITIZE TOILET ★ VACUUM OR MOP ★ WASH SHOWER,SINK AND MIRRORS ★ WASH TOWELS AND MATS ★
FRI	DINING	★ CLEAN OFF TABLE ★ VACUUM OR MOP ★ DUST SURFACES ★ PICK UP CLUTTER ★
SAT	ENTRY	★ SANTIZE DOORKNOBS ★ DUST SURFACES ★ VACUUM OR MOP ★ PUT AWAY SHOES/COATS/HATS ★
SUN	GROCERY	★ CLEAN OUT FRIDGE ★ MEAL PLAN ★ GROCERY SHOP AND FILL GAS TANK ★ MEAL PREP

DATE :

CLEANING CHEEKLIST

KEEP A GOOD THING GOING

EVERYDAY

	S	M	T	W	T	F	S
ONE LOAD OF LAUNDRY	◇	◇	◇	◇	◇	◇	◇
DISHES	◇	◇	◇	◇	◇	◇	◇
MAKE BEDS	◇	◇	◇	◇	◇	◇	◇
SPARY COUNTERTOPS	◇	◇	◇	◇	◇	◇	◇
PICK UP CLUTTER	◇	◇	◇	◇	◇	◇	◇
TRASH	◇	◇	◇	◇	◇	◇	◇
SORT MAIL	◇	◇	◇	◇	◇	◇	◇

MONTHLY

- ⬡ DUST CEILING FANS
- ⬡ CLEAN OVEN
- ⬡ CLEAN INSIDE OF FRIDGE
- ⬡ WASH WINDOWS
- ⬡ PICK UP GARAGE
- ⬡ PICK UP BASEMENT
- ⬡ DUST/CLEAN BASEBOARDS
- ⬡ GET RID OF ITEMS NO LONGER NEED
- ⬡ -----------------------------------
- ⬡ -----------------------------------
- ⬡ -----------------------------------
- ⬡ -----------------------------------

MON — KITCHEN
- ☆ CLEAN KITCHEN TABLE
- ☆ WIPE DOWN SINK AND COUNTERS
- ☆ VACUUM OR MOP
- ☆ WIPE DOWN APPLIANCES
- ☆

TUES — LIVING ROOM
- ☆ PICK UP CLUTTER
- ☆ VACUUM OR MOP
- ☆ WASH BLANKETS
- ☆ DUST SURFACES
- ☆

WED — BEDROOM
- ☆ PUT AWAY CLOTHES/PICK UP CLUTTER
- ☆ DUST SURFACES
- ☆ WASH BEDDING
- ☆ VACUUM OR MOP
- ☆

THUR — BATHROOM
- ☆ SANITIZE TOILET
- ☆ VACUUM OR MOP
- ☆ WASH SHOWER,SINK AND MIRRORS
- ☆ WASH TOWELS AND MATS
- ☆

FRI — DINING
- ☆ CLEAN OFF TABLE
- ☆ VACUUM OR MOP
- ☆ DUST SURFACES
- ☆ PICK UP CLUTTER
- ☆

SAT — ENTRY
- ☆ SANTIZE DOORKNOBS
- ☆ DUST SURFACES
- ☆ VACUUM OR MOP
- ☆ PUT AWAY SHOES/COATS/HATS
- ☆

SUN — GROCERY
- ☆ CLEAN OUT FRIDGE
- ☆ MEAL PLAN
- ☆ GROCERY SHOP AND FILL GAS TANK
- ☆ MEAL PREP
- ☆

DATE :

CLEANING CHEEKLIST

KEEP A GOOD THING GOING

EVERYDAY

	S	M	T	W	T	F	S
ONE LOAD OF LAUNDRY	◆	◆	◆	◆	◆	◆	◆
DISHES	◆	◆	◆	◆	◆	◆	◆
MAKE BEDS	◆	◆	◆	◆	◆	◆	◆
SPARY COUNTERTOPS	◆	◆	◆	◆	◆	◆	◆
PICK UP CLUTTER	◆	◆	◆	◆	◆	◆	◆
TRASH	◆	◆	◆	◆	◆	◆	◆
SORT MAIL	◆	◆	◆	◆	◆	◆	◆

MONTHLY

- ⬣ DUST CEILING FANS
- ⬣ CLEAN OVEN
- ⬣ CLEAN INSIDE OF FRIDGE
- ⬣ WASH WINDOWS
- ⬣ PICK UP GARAGE
- ⬣ PICK UP BASEMENT
- ⬣ DUST/CLEAN BASEBOARDS
- ⬣ GET RID OF ITEMS NO LONGER NEED
- ⬣ --------------------------------
- ⬣ --------------------------------
- ⬣ --------------------------------
- ⬣

MON — KITCHEN
- ★ CLEAN KITCHEN TABLE
- ★ WIPE DOWN SINK AND COUNTERS
- ★ VACUUM OR MOP
- ★ WIPE DOWN APPLIANCES
- ★

TUES — LIVINGROOM
- ★ PICK UP CLUTTER
- ★ VACUUM OR MOP
- ★ WASH BLANKETS
- ★ DUST SURFACES
- ★

WED — BEDROOM
- ★ PUT AWAY CLOTHES/PICK UP CLUTTER
- ★ DUST SURFACES
- ★ WASH BEDDING
- ★ VACUUM OR MOP
- ★

THUR — BATHROOM
- ★ SANITIZE TOILET
- ★ VACUUM OR MOP
- ★ WASH SHOWER,SINK AND MIRRORS
- ★ WASH TOWELS AND MATS
- ★

FRI — DINING
- ★ CLEAN OFF TABLE
- ★ VACUUM OR MOP
- ★ DUST SURFACES
- ★ PICK UP CLUTTER
- ★

SAT — ENTRY
- ★ SANTIZE DOORKNOBS
- ★ DUST SURFACES
- ★ VACUUM OR MOP
- ★ PUT AWAY SHOES/COATS/HATS
- ★

SUN — GROCERY
- ★ CLEAN OUT FRIDGE
- ★ MEAL PLAN
- ★ GROCERY SHOP AND FILL GAS TANK
- ★ MEAL PREP
- ★

DATE :

CLEANING CHEEKLIST

KEEP A GOOD THING GOING

EVERYDAY

	S	M	T	W	T	F	S
ONE LOAD OF LAUNDRY	◆	◆	◆	◆	◆	◆	◆
DISHES	◆	◆	◆	◆	◆	◆	◆
MAKE BEDS	◆	◆	◆	◆	◆	◆	◆
SPARY COUNTERTOPS	◆	◆	◆	◆	◆	◆	◆
PICK UP CLUTTER	◆	◆	◆	◆	◆	◆	◆
TRASH	◆	◆	◆	◆	◆	◆	◆
SORT MAIL	◆	◆	◆	◆	◆	◆	◆

MONTHLY

- DUST CEILING FANS
- CLEAN OVEN
- CLEAN INSIDE OF FRIDGE
- WASH WINDOWS
- PICK UP GARAGE
- PICK UP BASEMENT
- DUST/CLEAN BASEBOARDS
- GET RID OF ITEMS NO LONGER NEED
- _____
- _____
- _____
-

MON — **KITCHEN**
- ★ CLEAN KITCHEN TABLE
- ★ WIPE DOWN SINK AND COUNTERS
- ★ VACUUM OR MOP
- ★ WIPE DOWN APPLIANCES
- ★

TUES — **LIVINGROOM**
- ★ PICK UP CLUTTER
- ★ VACUUM OR MOP
- ★ WASH BLANKETS
- ★ DUST SURFACES
- ★

WED — **BEDROOM**
- ★ PUT AWAY CLOTHES/PICK UP CLUTTER
- ★ DUST SURFACES
- ★ WASH BEDDING
- ★ VACUUM OR MOP
- ★

THUR — **BATHROOM**
- ★ SANITIZE TOILET
- ★ VACUUM OR MOP
- ★ WASH SHOWER,SINK AND MIRRORS
- ★ WASH TOWELS AND MATS
- ★

FRI — **DINING**
- ★ CLEAN OFF TABLE
- ★ VACUUM OR MOP
- ★ DUST SURFACES
- ★ PICK UP CLUTTER
- ★

SAT — **ENTRY**
- ★ SANTIZE DOORKNOBS
- ★ DUST SURFACES
- ★ VACUUM OR MOP
- ★ PUT AWAY SHOES/COATS/HATS
- ★

SUN — **GROCERY**
- ★ CLEAN OUT FRIDGE
- ★ MEAL PLAN
- ★ GROCERY SHOP AND FILL GAS TANK
- ★ MEAL PREP
- ★

DATE :

CLEANING CHEEKLIST

KEEP A GOOD THING GOING

EVERYDAY

	S	M	T	W	T	F	S
ONE LOAD OF LAUNDRY	◆	◆	◆	◆	◆	◆	◆
DISHES	◆	◆	◆	◆	◆	◆	◆
MAKE BEDS	◆	◆	◆	◆	◆	◆	◆
SPARY COUNTERTOPS	◆	◆	◆	◆	◆	◆	◆
PICK UP CLUTTER	◆	◆	◆	◆	◆	◆	◆
TRASH	◆	◆	◆	◆	◆	◆	◆
SORT MAIL	◆	◆	◆	◆	◆	◆	◆

MONTHLY

- ⬡ DUST CEILING FANS
- ⬡ CLEAN OVEN
- ⬡ CLEAN INSIDE OF FRIDGE
- ⬡ WASH WINDOWS
- ⬡ PICK UP GARAGE
- ⬡ PICK UP BASEMENT
- ⬡ DUST/CLEAN BASEBOARDS
- ⬡ GET RID OF ITEMS NO LONGER NEED
- ⬡ _____
- ⬡ _____
- ⬡ _____
- ⬡

MON	KITCHEN	☆ CLEAN KITCHEN TABLE ☆ WIPE DOWN SINK AND COUNTERS ☆ VACUUM OR MOP ☆ WIPE DOWN APPLIANCES ☆
TUES	LIVINGROOM	☆ PICK UP CLUTTER ☆ VACUUM OR MOP ☆ WASH BLANKETS ☆ DUST SURFACES ☆
WED	BEDROOM	☆ PUT AWAY CLOTHES/PICK UP CLUTTER ☆ DUST SURFACES ☆ WASH BEDDING ☆ VACUUM OR MOP ☆
THUR	BATHROOM	☆ SANITIZE TOILET ☆ VACUUM OR MOP ☆ WASH SHOWER,SINK AND MIRRORS ☆ WASH TOWELS AND MATS ☆
FRI	DINING	☆ CLEAN OFF TABLE ☆ VACUUM OR MOP ☆ DUST SURFACES ☆ PICK UP CLUTTER
SAT	ENTRY	☆ SANTIZE DOORKNOBS ☆ DUST SURFACES ☆ VACUUM OR MOP ☆ PUT AWAY SHOES/COATS/HATS ☆
SUN	GROCERY	☆ CLEAN OUT FRIDGE ☆ MEAL PLAN ☆ GROCERY SHOP AND FILL GAS TANK ☆ MEAL PREP ☆

DATE :

CLEANING CHEEKLIST

KEEP A GOOD THING GOING

EVERYDAY

	S	M	T	W	T	F	S
ONE LOAD OF LAUNDRY	◆	◆	◆	◆	◆	◆	◆
DISHES	◆	◆	◆	◆	◆	◆	◆
MAKE BEDS	◆	◆	◆	◆	◆	◆	◆
SPARY COUNTERTOPS	◆	◆	◆	◆	◆	◆	◆
PICK UP CLUTTER	◆	◆	◆	◆	◆	◆	◆
TRASH	◆	◆	◆	◆	◆	◆	◆
SORT MAIL	◆	◆	◆	◆	◆	◆	◆

MONTHLY

- DUST CEILING FANS
- CLEAN OVEN
- CLEAN INSIDE OF FRIDGE
- WASH WINDOWS
- PICK UP GARAGE
- PICK UP BASEMENT
- DUST/CLEAN BASEBOARDS
- GET RID OF ITEMS NO LONGER NEED
- _____
- _____
- _____
- _____

MON — KITCHEN
- ★ CLEAN KITCHEN TABLE
- ★ WIPE DOWN SINK AND COUNTERS
- ★ VACUUM OR MOP
- ★ WIPE DOWN APPLIANCES
- ★

TUES — LIVINGROOM
- ★ PICK UP CLUTTER
- ★ VACUUM OR MOP
- ★ WASH BLANKETS
- ★ DUST SURFACES
- ★

WED — BEDROOM
- ★ PUT AWAY CLOTHES/PICK UP CLUTTER
- ★ DUST SURFACES
- ★ WASH BEDDING
- ★ VACUUM OR MOP
- ★

THUR — BATHROOM
- ★ SANITIZE TOILET
- ★ VACUUM OR MOP
- ★ WASH SHOWER,SINK AND MIRRORS
- ★ WASH TOWELS AND MATS
- ★

FRI — DINING
- ★ CLEAN OFF TABLE
- ★ VACUUM OR MOP
- ★ DUST SURFACES
- ★ PICK UP CLUTTER
- ★

SAT — ENTRY
- ★ SANTIZE DOORKNOBS
- ★ DUST SURFACES
- ★ VACUUM OR MOP
- ★ PUT AWAY SHOES/COATS/HATS
- ★

SUN — GROCERY
- ★ CLEAN OUT FRIDGE
- ★ MEAL PLAN
- ★ GROCERY SHOP AND FILL GAS TANK
- ★ MEAL PREP
- ★

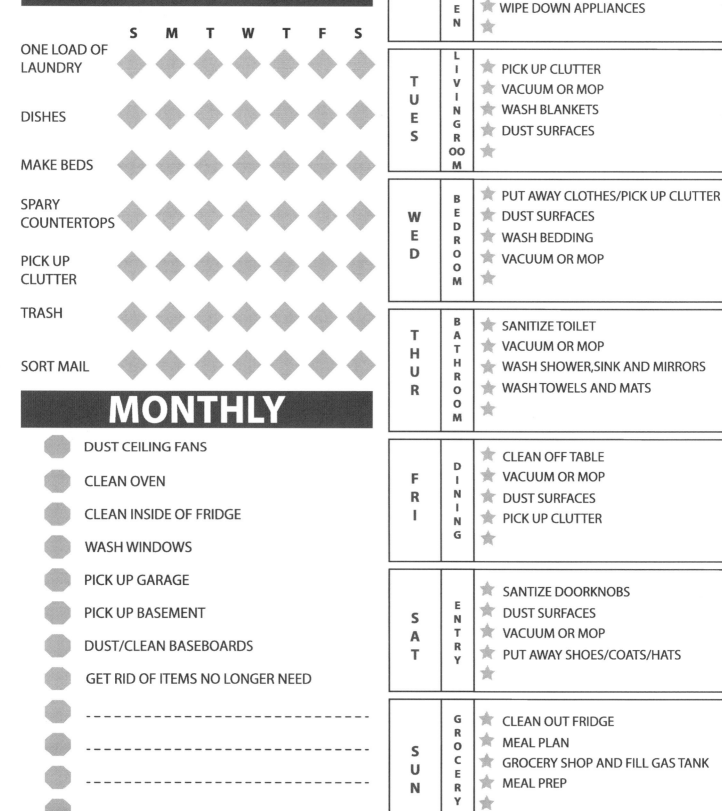

DATE :   CLEANING CHEEKLIST

KEEP A GOOD THING GOING

EVERYDAY

	S	M	T	W	T	F	S
ONE LOAD OF LAUNDRY	◆	◆	◆	◆	◆	◆	◆
DISHES	◆	◆	◆	◆	◆	◆	◆
MAKE BEDS	◆	◆	◆	◆	◆	◆	◆
SPARY COUNTERTOPS	◆	◆	◆	◆	◆	◆	◆
PICK UP CLUTTER	◆	◆	◆	◆	◆	◆	◆
TRASH	◆	◆	◆	◆	◆	◆	◆
SORT MAIL	◆	◆	◆	◆	◆	◆	◆

MONTHLY

- DUST CEILING FANS
- CLEAN OVEN
- CLEAN INSIDE OF FRIDGE
- WASH WINDOWS
- PICK UP GARAGE
- PICK UP BASEMENT
- DUST/CLEAN BASEBOARDS
- GET RID OF ITEMS NO LONGER NEED
- _____
- _____
- _____
- _____

MON	KITCHEN	☆ CLEAN KITCHEN TABLE ☆ WIPE DOWN SINK AND COUNTERS ☆ VACUUM OR MOP ☆ WIPE DOWN APPLIANCES ☆
TUES	LIVINGROOM	☆ PICK UP CLUTTER ☆ VACUUM OR MOP ☆ WASH BLANKETS ☆ DUST SURFACES ☆
WED	BEDROOM	☆ PUT AWAY CLOTHES/PICK UP CLUTTER ☆ DUST SURFACES ☆ WASH BEDDING ☆ VACUUM OR MOP ☆
THUR	BATHROOM	☆ SANITIZE TOILET ☆ VACUUM OR MOP ☆ WASH SHOWER,SINK AND MIRRORS ☆ WASH TOWELS AND MATS ☆
FRI	DINING	☆ CLEAN OFF TABLE ☆ VACUUM OR MOP ☆ DUST SURFACES ☆ PICK UP CLUTTER ☆
SAT	ENTRY	☆ SANTIZE DOORKNOBS ☆ DUST SURFACES ☆ VACUUM OR MOP ☆ PUT AWAY SHOES/COATS/HATS ☆
SUN	GROCERY	☆ CLEAN OUT FRIDGE ☆ MEAL PLAN ☆ GROCERY SHOP AND FILL GAS TANK ☆ MEAL PREP ☆

DATE :

CLEANING CHEEKLIST

KEEP A GOOD THING GOING

EVERYDAY

	S	M	T	W	T	F	S
ONE LOAD OF LAUNDRY	◆	◆	◆	◆	◆	◆	◆
DISHES	◆	◆	◆	◆	◆	◆	◆
MAKE BEDS	◆	◆	◆	◆	◆	◆	◆
SPARY COUNTERTOPS	◆	◆	◆	◆	◆	◆	◆
PICK UP CLUTTER	◆	◆	◆	◆	◆	◆	◆
TRASH	◆	◆	◆	◆	◆	◆	◆
SORT MAIL	◆	◆	◆	◆	◆	◆	◆

MONTHLY

- DUST CEILING FANS
- CLEAN OVEN
- CLEAN INSIDE OF FRIDGE
- WASH WINDOWS
- PICK UP GARAGE
- PICK UP BASEMENT
- DUST/CLEAN BASEBOARDS
- GET RID OF ITEMS NO LONGER NEED
- _____
- _____
- _____
- _____

MON — KITCHEN
- ★ CLEAN KITCHEN TABLE
- ★ WIPE DOWN SINK AND COUNTERS
- ★ VACUUM OR MOP
- ★ WIPE DOWN APPLIANCES
- ★

TUES — LIVINGROOM
- ★ PICK UP CLUTTER
- ★ VACUUM OR MOP
- ★ WASH BLANKETS
- ★ DUST SURFACES
- ★

WED — BEDROOM
- ★ PUT AWAY CLOTHES/PICK UP CLUTTER
- ★ DUST SURFACES
- ★ WASH BEDDING
- ★ VACUUM OR MOP
- ★

THUR — BATHROOM
- ★ SANITIZE TOILET
- ★ VACUUM OR MOP
- ★ WASH SHOWER,SINK AND MIRRORS
- ★ WASH TOWELS AND MATS
- ★

FRI — DINING
- ★ CLEAN OFF TABLE
- ★ VACUUM OR MOP
- ★ DUST SURFACES
- ★ PICK UP CLUTTER
- ★

SAT — ENTRY
- ★ SANTIZE DOORKNOBS
- ★ DUST SURFACES
- ★ VACUUM OR MOP
- ★ PUT AWAY SHOES/COATS/HATS
- ★

SUN — GROCERY
- ★ CLEAN OUT FRIDGE
- ★ MEAL PLAN
- ★ GROCERY SHOP AND FILL GAS TANK
- ★ MEAL PREP
- ★

DATE :

CLEANING CHEEKLIST

KEEP A GOOD THING GOING

EVERYDAY

	S	M	T	W	T	F	S
ONE LOAD OF LAUNDRY	◆	◆	◆	◆	◆	◆	◆
DISHES	◆	◆	◆	◆	◆	◆	◆
MAKE BEDS	◆	◆	◆	◆	◆	◆	◆
SPARY COUNTERTOPS	◆	◆	◆	◆	◆	◆	◆
PICK UP CLUTTER	◆	◆	◆	◆	◆	◆	◆
TRASH	◆	◆	◆	◆	◆	◆	◆
SORT MAIL	◆	◆	◆	◆	◆	◆	◆

MONTHLY

- DUST CEILING FANS
- CLEAN OVEN
- CLEAN INSIDE OF FRIDGE
- WASH WINDOWS
- PICK UP GARAGE
- PICK UP BASEMENT
- DUST/CLEAN BASEBOARDS
- GET RID OF ITEMS NO LONGER NEED
- -
- -
- -

MON	KITCHEN	☆ CLEAN KITCHEN TABLE ☆ WIPE DOWN SINK AND COUNTERS ☆ VACUUM OR MOP ☆ WIPE DOWN APPLIANCES ☆
TUES	LIVINGROOM	☆ PICK UP CLUTTER ☆ VACUUM OR MOP ☆ WASH BLANKETS ☆ DUST SURFACES ☆
WED	BEDROOM	☆ PUT AWAY CLOTHES/PICK UP CLUTTER ☆ DUST SURFACES ☆ WASH BEDDING ☆ VACUUM OR MOP ☆
THUR	BATHROOM	☆ SANITIZE TOILET ☆ VACUUM OR MOP ☆ WASH SHOWER,SINK AND MIRRORS ☆ WASH TOWELS AND MATS ☆
FRI	DINING	☆ CLEAN OFF TABLE ☆ VACUUM OR MOP ☆ DUST SURFACES ☆ PICK UP CLUTTER ☆
SAT	ENTRY	☆ SANTIZE DOORKNOBS ☆ DUST SURFACES ☆ VACUUM OR MOP ☆ PUT AWAY SHOES/COATS/HATS ☆
SUN	GROCERY	☆ CLEAN OUT FRIDGE ☆ MEAL PLAN ☆ GROCERY SHOP AND FILL GAS TANK ☆ MEAL PREP ☆

DATE :

CLEANING CHEEKLIST

KEEP A GOOD THING GOING

EVERYDAY

	S	M	T	W	T	F	S
ONE LOAD OF LAUNDRY	◆	◆	◆	◆	◆	◆	◆
DISHES	◆	◆	◆	◆	◆	◆	◆
MAKE BEDS	◆	◆	◆	◆	◆	◆	◆
SPARY COUNTERTOPS	◆	◆	◆	◆	◆	◆	◆
PICK UP CLUTTER	◆	◆	◆	◆	◆	◆	◆
TRASH	◆	◆	◆	◆	◆	◆	◆
SORT MAIL	◆	◆	◆	◆	◆	◆	◆

MONTHLY

- DUST CEILING FANS
- CLEAN OVEN
- CLEAN INSIDE OF FRIDGE
- WASH WINDOWS
- PICK UP GARAGE
- PICK UP BASEMENT
- DUST/CLEAN BASEBOARDS
- GET RID OF ITEMS NO LONGER NEED
- _____
- _____
- _____
- _____

MON — **KITCHEN**
- ★ CLEAN KITCHEN TABLE
- ★ WIPE DOWN SINK AND COUNTERS
- ★ VACUUM OR MOP
- ★ WIPE DOWN APPLIANCES
- ★

TUES — **LIVINGROOM**
- ★ PICK UP CLUTTER
- ★ VACUUM OR MOP
- ★ WASH BLANKETS
- ★ DUST SURFACES
- ★

WED — **BEDROOM**
- ★ PUT AWAY CLOTHES/PICK UP CLUTTER
- ★ DUST SURFACES
- ★ WASH BEDDING
- ★ VACUUM OR MOP
- ★

THUR — **BATHROOM**
- ★ SANITIZE TOILET
- ★ VACUUM OR MOP
- ★ WASH SHOWER,SINK AND MIRRORS
- ★ WASH TOWELS AND MATS
- ★

FRI — **DINING**
- ★ CLEAN OFF TABLE
- ★ VACUUM OR MOP
- ★ DUST SURFACES
- ★ PICK UP CLUTTER
- ★

SAT — **ENTRY**
- ★ SANTIZE DOORKNOBS
- ★ DUST SURFACES
- ★ VACUUM OR MOP
- ★ PUT AWAY SHOES/COATS/HATS
- ★

SUN — **GROCERY**
- ★ CLEAN OUT FRIDGE
- ★ MEAL PLAN
- ★ GROCERY SHOP AND FILL GAS TANK
- ★ MEAL PREP
- ★

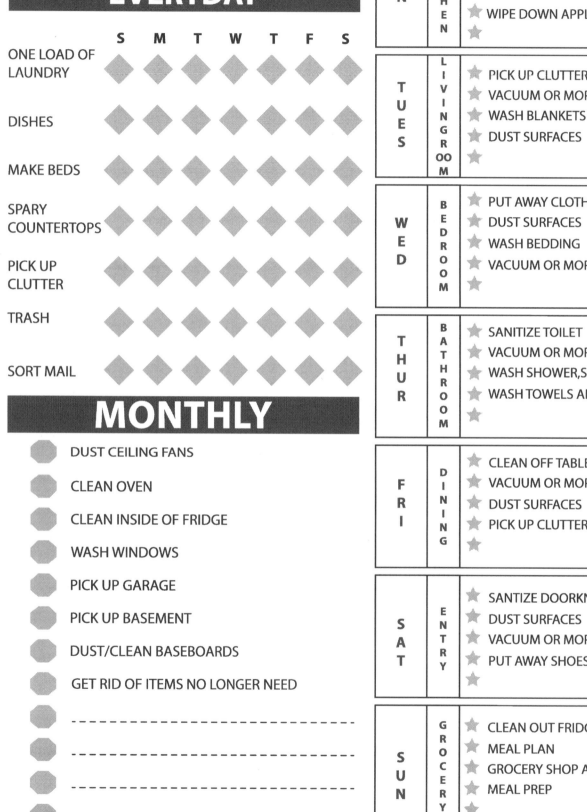

DATE :

CLEANING CHEEKLIST

KEEP A GOOD THING GOING

EVERYDAY

	S	M	T	W	T	F	S
ONE LOAD OF LAUNDRY	◆	◆	◆	◆	◆	◆	◆
DISHES	◆	◆	◆	◆	◆	◆	◆
MAKE BEDS	◆	◆	◆	◆	◆	◆	◆
SPARY COUNTERTOPS	◆	◆	◆	◆	◆	◆	◆
PICK UP CLUTTER	◆	◆	◆	◆	◆	◆	◆
TRASH	◆	◆	◆	◆	◆	◆	◆
SORT MAIL	◆	◆	◆	◆	◆	◆	◆

MONTHLY

- DUST CEILING FANS
- CLEAN OVEN
- CLEAN INSIDE OF FRIDGE
- WASH WINDOWS
- PICK UP GARAGE
- PICK UP BASEMENT
- DUST/CLEAN BASEBOARDS
- GET RID OF ITEMS NO LONGER NEED
- ------------------------------
- ------------------------------
- ------------------------------
- ------------------------------

MON	KITCHEN	★ CLEAN KITCHEN TABLE ★ WIPE DOWN SINK AND COUNTERS ★ VACUUM OR MOP ★ WIPE DOWN APPLIANCES ★
TUES	LIVINGROOM	★ PICK UP CLUTTER ★ VACUUM OR MOP ★ WASH BLANKETS ★ DUST SURFACES ★
WED	BEDROOM	★ PUT AWAY CLOTHES/PICK UP CLUTTER ★ DUST SURFACES ★ WASH BEDDING ★ VACUUM OR MOP ★
THUR	BATHROOM	★ SANITIZE TOILET ★ VACUUM OR MOP ★ WASH SHOWER,SINK AND MIRRORS ★ WASH TOWELS AND MATS ★
FRI	DINING	★ CLEAN OFF TABLE ★ VACUUM OR MOP ★ DUST SURFACES ★ PICK UP CLUTTER ★
SAT	ENTRY	★ SANTIZE DOORKNOBS ★ DUST SURFACES ★ VACUUM OR MOP ★ PUT AWAY SHOES/COATS/HATS ★
SUN	GROCERY	★ CLEAN OUT FRIDGE ★ MEAL PLAN ★ GROCERY SHOP AND FILL GAS TANK ★ MEAL PREP ★

DATE :   CLEANING CHEEKLIST

KEEP A GOOD THING GOING

EVERYDAY

	S	M	T	W	T	F	S
ONE LOAD OF LAUNDRY	◆	◆	◆	◆	◆	◆	◆
DISHES	◆	◆	◆	◆	◆	◆	◆
MAKE BEDS	◆	◆	◆	◆	◆	◆	◆
SPARY COUNTERTOPS	◆	◆	◆	◆	◆	◆	◆
PICK UP CLUTTER	◆	◆	◆	◆	◆	◆	◆
TRASH	◆	◆	◆	◆	◆	◆	◆
SORT MAIL	◆	◆	◆	◆	◆	◆	◆

MONTHLY

- DUST CEILING FANS
- CLEAN OVEN
- CLEAN INSIDE OF FRIDGE
- WASH WINDOWS
- PICK UP GARAGE
- PICK UP BASEMENT
- DUST/CLEAN BASEBOARDS
- GET RID OF ITEMS NO LONGER NEED
- _____
- _____
- _____
- _____

MON — KITCHEN
- ⭐ CLEAN KITCHEN TABLE
- ⭐ WIPE DOWN SINK AND COUNTERS
- ⭐ VACUUM OR MOP
- ⭐ WIPE DOWN APPLIANCES
- ⭐

TUES — LIVING ROOM
- ⭐ PICK UP CLUTTER
- ⭐ VACUUM OR MOP
- ⭐ WASH BLANKETS
- ⭐ DUST SURFACES
- ⭐

WED — BEDROOM
- ⭐ PUT AWAY CLOTHES/PICK UP CLUTTER
- ⭐ DUST SURFACES
- ⭐ WASH BEDDING
- ⭐ VACUUM OR MOP
- ⭐

THUR — BATHROOM
- ⭐ SANITIZE TOILET
- ⭐ VACUUM OR MOP
- ⭐ WASH SHOWER, SINK AND MIRRORS
- ⭐ WASH TOWELS AND MATS
- ⭐

FRI — DINING
- ⭐ CLEAN OFF TABLE
- ⭐ VACUUM OR MOP
- ⭐ DUST SURFACES
- ⭐ PICK UP CLUTTER
- ⭐

SAT — ENTRY
- ⭐ SANTIZE DOORKNOBS
- ⭐ DUST SURFACES
- ⭐ VACUUM OR MOP
- ⭐ PUT AWAY SHOES/COATS/HATS
- ⭐

SUN — GROCERY
- ⭐ CLEAN OUT FRIDGE
- ⭐ MEAL PLAN
- ⭐ GROCERY SHOP AND FILL GAS TANK
- ⭐ MEAL PREP
- ⭐

DATE :   CLEANING CHEEKLIST

KEEP A GOOD THING GOING

EVERYDAY

	S	M	T	W	T	F	S
ONE LOAD OF LAUNDRY	◆	◆	◆	◆	◆	◆	◆
DISHES	◆	◆	◆	◆	◆	◆	◆
MAKE BEDS	◆	◆	◆	◆	◆	◆	◆
SPARY COUNTERTOPS	◆	◆	◆	◆	◆	◆	◆
PICK UP CLUTTER	◆	◆	◆	◆	◆	◆	◆
TRASH	◆	◆	◆	◆	◆	◆	◆
SORT MAIL	◆	◆	◆	◆	◆	◆	◆

MONTHLY

- DUST CEILING FANS
- CLEAN OVEN
- CLEAN INSIDE OF FRIDGE
- WASH WINDOWS
- PICK UP GARAGE
- PICK UP BASEMENT
- DUST/CLEAN BASEBOARDS
- GET RID OF ITEMS NO LONGER NEED
- -
- -
- -
-

MON	KITCHEN	★ CLEAN KITCHEN TABLE ★ WIPE DOWN SINK AND COUNTERS ★ VACUUM OR MOP ★ WIPE DOWN APPLIANCES ★
TUES	LIVINGROOM	★ PICK UP CLUTTER ★ VACUUM OR MOP ★ WASH BLANKETS ★ DUST SURFACES ★
WED	BEDROOM	★ PUT AWAY CLOTHES/PICK UP CLUTTER ★ DUST SURFACES ★ WASH BEDDING ★ VACUUM OR MOP ★
THUR	BATHROOM	★ SANITIZE TOILET ★ VACUUM OR MOP ★ WASH SHOWER,SINK AND MIRRORS ★ WASH TOWELS AND MATS ★
FRI	DINING	★ CLEAN OFF TABLE ★ VACUUM OR MOP ★ DUST SURFACES ★ PICK UP CLUTTER ★
SAT	ENTRY	★ SANTIZE DOORKNOBS ★ DUST SURFACES ★ VACUUM OR MOP ★ PUT AWAY SHOES/COATS/HATS ★
SUN	GROCERY	★ CLEAN OUT FRIDGE ★ MEAL PLAN ★ GROCERY SHOP AND FILL GAS TANK ★ MEAL PREP

DATE :   CLEANING CHEEKLIST

KEEP A GOOD THING GOING

EVERYDAY

	S	M	T	W	T	F	S
ONE LOAD OF LAUNDRY	◆	◆	◆	◆	◆	◆	◆
DISHES	◆	◆	◆	◆	◆	◆	◆
MAKE BEDS	◆	◆	◆	◆	◆	◆	◆
SPARY COUNTERTOPS	◆	◆	◆	◆	◆	◆	◆
PICK UP CLUTTER	◆	◆	◆	◆	◆	◆	◆
TRASH	◆	◆	◆	◆	◆	◆	◆
SORT MAIL	◆	◆	◆	◆	◆	◆	◆

MONTHLY

- ⬡ DUST CEILING FANS
- ⬡ CLEAN OVEN
- ⬡ CLEAN INSIDE OF FRIDGE
- ⬡ WASH WINDOWS
- ⬡ PICK UP GARAGE
- ⬡ PICK UP BASEMENT
- ⬡ DUST/CLEAN BASEBOARDS
- ⬡ GET RID OF ITEMS NO LONGER NEED
- ⬡ -----------------------------
- ⬡ -----------------------------
- ⬡ -----------------------------
- ⬡ -----------------------------

MON	KITCHEN	
		★ CLEAN KITCHEN TABLE
		★ WIPE DOWN SINK AND COUNTERS
		★ VACUUM OR MOP
		★ WIPE DOWN APPLIANCES
		★

TUES	LIVINGROOM	
		★ PICK UP CLUTTER
		★ VACUUM OR MOP
		★ WASH BLANKETS
		★ DUST SURFACES
		★

WED	BEDROOM	
		★ PUT AWAY CLOTHES/PICK UP CLUTTER
		★ DUST SURFACES
		★ WASH BEDDING
		★ VACUUM OR MOP
		★

THUR	BATHROOM	
		★ SANITIZE TOILET
		★ VACUUM OR MOP
		★ WASH SHOWER,SINK AND MIRRORS
		★ WASH TOWELS AND MATS
		★

FRI	DINING	
		★ CLEAN OFF TABLE
		★ VACUUM OR MOP
		★ DUST SURFACES
		★ PICK UP CLUTTER
		★

SAT	ENTRY	
		★ SANTIZE DOORKNOBS
		★ DUST SURFACES
		★ VACUUM OR MOP
		★ PUT AWAY SHOES/COATS/HATS
		★

SUN	GROCERY	
		★ CLEAN OUT FRIDGE
		★ MEAL PLAN
		★ GROCERY SHOP AND FILL GAS TANK
		★ MEAL PREP
		★

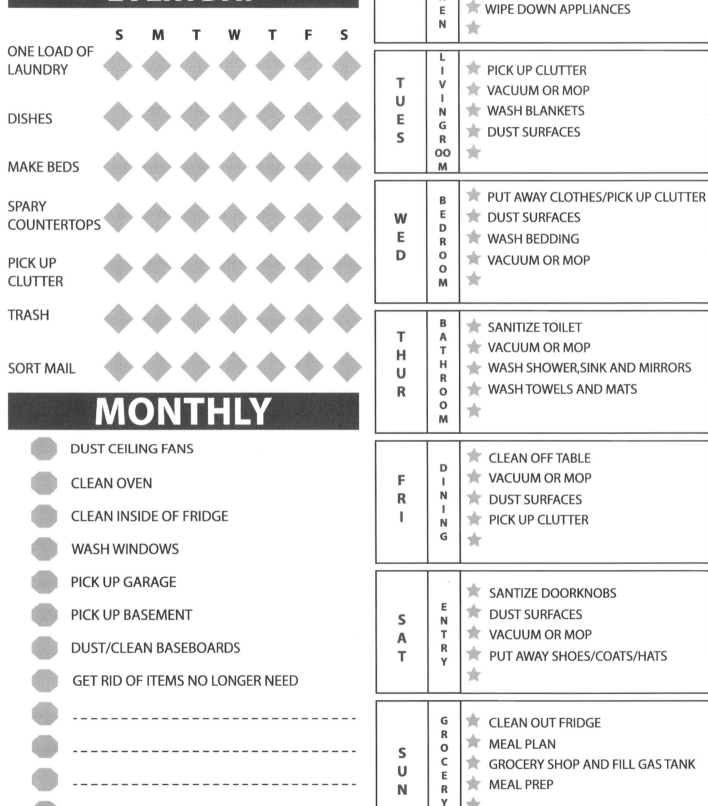

DATE :

CLEANING CHEEKLIST

KEEP A GOOD THING GOING

EVERYDAY

	S	M	T	W	T	F	S
ONE LOAD OF LAUNDRY	◆	◆	◆	◆	◆	◆	◆
DISHES	◆	◆	◆	◆	◆	◆	◆
MAKE BEDS	◆	◆	◆	◆	◆	◆	◆
SPARY COUNTERTOPS	◆	◆	◆	◆	◆	◆	◆
PICK UP CLUTTER	◆	◆	◆	◆	◆	◆	◆
TRASH	◆	◆	◆	◆	◆	◆	◆
SORT MAIL	◆	◆	◆	◆	◆	◆	◆

MONTHLY

- DUST CEILING FANS
- CLEAN OVEN
- CLEAN INSIDE OF FRIDGE
- WASH WINDOWS
- PICK UP GARAGE
- PICK UP BASEMENT
- DUST/CLEAN BASEBOARDS
- GET RID OF ITEMS NO LONGER NEED
- _____
- _____
- _____
- _____

MON	KITCHEN	★ CLEAN KITCHEN TABLE ★ WIPE DOWN SINK AND COUNTERS ★ VACUUM OR MOP ★ WIPE DOWN APPLIANCES ★
TUES	LIVING ROOM	★ PICK UP CLUTTER ★ VACUUM OR MOP ★ WASH BLANKETS ★ DUST SURFACES ★
WED	BEDROOM	★ PUT AWAY CLOTHES/PICK UP CLUTTER ★ DUST SURFACES ★ WASH BEDDING ★ VACUUM OR MOP ★
THUR	BATHROOM	★ SANITIZE TOILET ★ VACUUM OR MOP ★ WASH SHOWER,SINK AND MIRRORS ★ WASH TOWELS AND MATS ★
FRI	DINING	★ CLEAN OFF TABLE ★ VACUUM OR MOP ★ DUST SURFACES ★ PICK UP CLUTTER ★
SAT	ENTRY	★ SANTIZE DOORKNOBS ★ DUST SURFACES ★ VACUUM OR MOP ★ PUT AWAY SHOES/COATS/HATS ★
SUN	GROCERY	★ CLEAN OUT FRIDGE ★ MEAL PLAN ★ GROCERY SHOP AND FILL GAS TANK ★ MEAL PREP ★

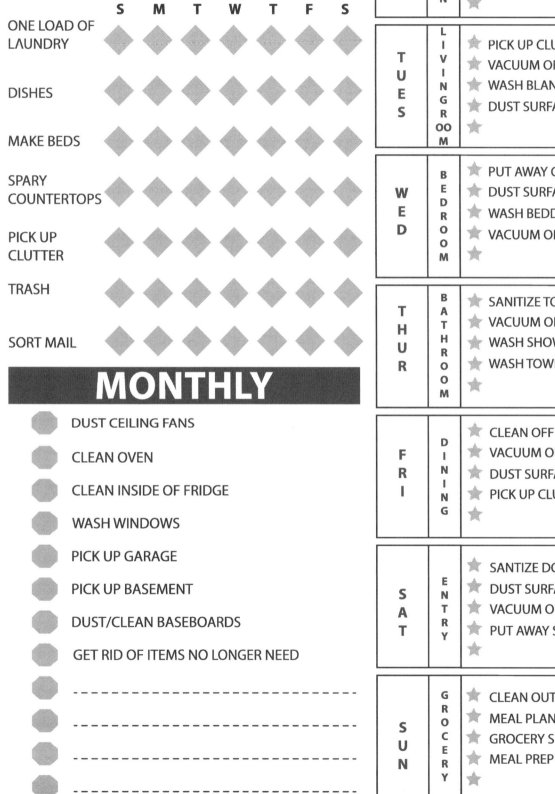

DATE :

CLEANING CHEEKLIST

KEEP A GOOD THING GOING

EVERYDAY

	S	M	T	W	T	F	S
ONE LOAD OF LAUNDRY	◆	◆	◆	◆	◆	◆	◆
DISHES	◆	◆	◆	◆	◆	◆	◆
MAKE BEDS	◆	◆	◆	◆	◆	◆	◆
SPARY COUNTERTOPS	◆	◆	◆	◆	◆	◆	◆
PICK UP CLUTTER	◆	◆	◆	◆	◆	◆	◆
TRASH	◆	◆	◆	◆	◆	◆	◆
SORT MAIL	◆	◆	◆	◆	◆	◆	◆

MONTHLY

- DUST CEILING FANS
- CLEAN OVEN
- CLEAN INSIDE OF FRIDGE
- WASH WINDOWS
- PICK UP GARAGE
- PICK UP BASEMENT
- DUST/CLEAN BASEBOARDS
- GET RID OF ITEMS NO LONGER NEED
- -
- -
- -
- -

MON — KITCHEN
- ★ CLEAN KITCHEN TABLE
- ★ WIPE DOWN SINK AND COUNTERS
- ★ VACUUM OR MOP
- ★ WIPE DOWN APPLIANCES
- ★

TUES — LIVINGROOM
- ★ PICK UP CLUTTER
- ★ VACUUM OR MOP
- ★ WASH BLANKETS
- ★ DUST SURFACES
- ★

WED — BEDROOM
- ★ PUT AWAY CLOTHES/PICK UP CLUTTER
- ★ DUST SURFACES
- ★ WASH BEDDING
- ★ VACUUM OR MOP
- ★

THUR — BATHROOM
- ★ SANITIZE TOILET
- ★ VACUUM OR MOP
- ★ WASH SHOWER,SINK AND MIRRORS
- ★ WASH TOWELS AND MATS
- ★

FRI — DINING
- ★ CLEAN OFF TABLE
- ★ VACUUM OR MOP
- ★ DUST SURFACES
- ★ PICK UP CLUTTER
- ★

SAT — ENTRY
- ★ SANTIZE DOORKNOBS
- ★ DUST SURFACES
- ★ VACUUM OR MOP
- ★ PUT AWAY SHOES/COATS/HATS
- ★

SUN — GROCERY
- ★ CLEAN OUT FRIDGE
- ★ MEAL PLAN
- ★ GROCERY SHOP AND FILL GAS TANK
- ★ MEAL PREP
- ★

DATE :

CLEANING CHEEKLIST

KEEP A GOOD THING GOING

EVERYDAY

	S	M	T	W	T	F	S
ONE LOAD OF LAUNDRY	◆	◆	◆	◆	◆	◆	◆
DISHES	◆	◆	◆	◆	◆	◆	◆
MAKE BEDS	◆	◆	◆	◆	◆	◆	◆
SPARY COUNTERTOPS	◆	◆	◆	◆	◆	◆	◆
PICK UP CLUTTER	◆	◆	◆	◆	◆	◆	◆
TRASH	◆	◆	◆	◆	◆	◆	◆
SORT MAIL	◆	◆	◆	◆	◆	◆	◆

MONTHLY

- DUST CEILING FANS
- CLEAN OVEN
- CLEAN INSIDE OF FRIDGE
- WASH WINDOWS
- PICK UP GARAGE
- PICK UP BASEMENT
- DUST/CLEAN BASEBOARDS
- GET RID OF ITEMS NO LONGER NEED
- -
- -
- -
- -

MON — KITCHEN
- ★ CLEAN KITCHEN TABLE
- ★ WIPE DOWN SINK AND COUNTERS
- ★ VACUUM OR MOP
- ★ WIPE DOWN APPLIANCES
- ★

TUES — LIVINGROOM
- ★ PICK UP CLUTTER
- ★ VACUUM OR MOP
- ★ WASH BLANKETS
- ★ DUST SURFACES
- ★

WED — BEDROOM
- ★ PUT AWAY CLOTHES/PICK UP CLUTTER
- ★ DUST SURFACES
- ★ WASH BEDDING
- ★ VACUUM OR MOP
- ★

THUR — BATHROOM
- ★ SANITIZE TOILET
- ★ VACUUM OR MOP
- ★ WASH SHOWER,SINK AND MIRRORS
- ★ WASH TOWELS AND MATS
- ★

FRI — DINING
- ★ CLEAN OFF TABLE
- ★ VACUUM OR MOP
- ★ DUST SURFACES
- ★ PICK UP CLUTTER
- ★

SAT — ENTRY
- ★ SANTIZE DOORKNOBS
- ★ DUST SURFACES
- ★ VACUUM OR MOP
- ★ PUT AWAY SHOES/COATS/HATS
- ★

SUN — GROCERY
- ★ CLEAN OUT FRIDGE
- ★ MEAL PLAN
- ★ GROCERY SHOP AND FILL GAS TANK
- ★ MEAL PREP
- ★

DATE :

CLEANING CHEEKLIST

KEEP A GOOD THING GOING

EVERYDAY

	S	M	T	W	T	F	S
ONE LOAD OF LAUNDRY	◆	◆	◆	◆	◆	◆	◆
DISHES	◆	◆	◆	◆	◆	◆	◆
MAKE BEDS	◆	◆	◆	◆	◆	◆	◆
SPARY COUNTERTOPS	◆	◆	◆	◆	◆	◆	◆
PICK UP CLUTTER	◆	◆	◆	◆	◆	◆	◆
TRASH	◆	◆	◆	◆	◆	◆	◆
SORT MAIL	◆	◆	◆	◆	◆	◆	◆

MONTHLY

- DUST CEILING FANS
- CLEAN OVEN
- CLEAN INSIDE OF FRIDGE
- WASH WINDOWS
- PICK UP GARAGE
- PICK UP BASEMENT
- DUST/CLEAN BASEBOARDS
- GET RID OF ITEMS NO LONGER NEED
- _____
- _____
- _____
- _____

MON — KITCHEN
- ★ CLEAN KITCHEN TABLE
- ★ WIPE DOWN SINK AND COUNTERS
- ★ VACUUM OR MOP
- ★ WIPE DOWN APPLIANCES
- ★

TUES — LIVING ROOM
- ★ PICK UP CLUTTER
- ★ VACUUM OR MOP
- ★ WASH BLANKETS
- ★ DUST SURFACES
- ★

WED — BEDROOM
- ★ PUT AWAY CLOTHES/PICK UP CLUTTER
- ★ DUST SURFACES
- ★ WASH BEDDING
- ★ VACUUM OR MOP
- ★

THUR — BATHROOM
- ★ SANITIZE TOILET
- ★ VACUUM OR MOP
- ★ WASH SHOWER,SINK AND MIRRORS
- ★ WASH TOWELS AND MATS
- ★

FRI — DINING
- ★ CLEAN OFF TABLE
- ★ VACUUM OR MOP
- ★ DUST SURFACES
- ★ PICK UP CLUTTER
- ★

SAT — ENTRY
- ★ SANTIZE DOORKNOBS
- ★ DUST SURFACES
- ★ VACUUM OR MOP
- ★ PUT AWAY SHOES/COATS/HATS
- ★

SUN — GROCERY
- ★ CLEAN OUT FRIDGE
- ★ MEAL PLAN
- ★ GROCERY SHOP AND FILL GAS TANK
- ★ MEAL PREP
- ★

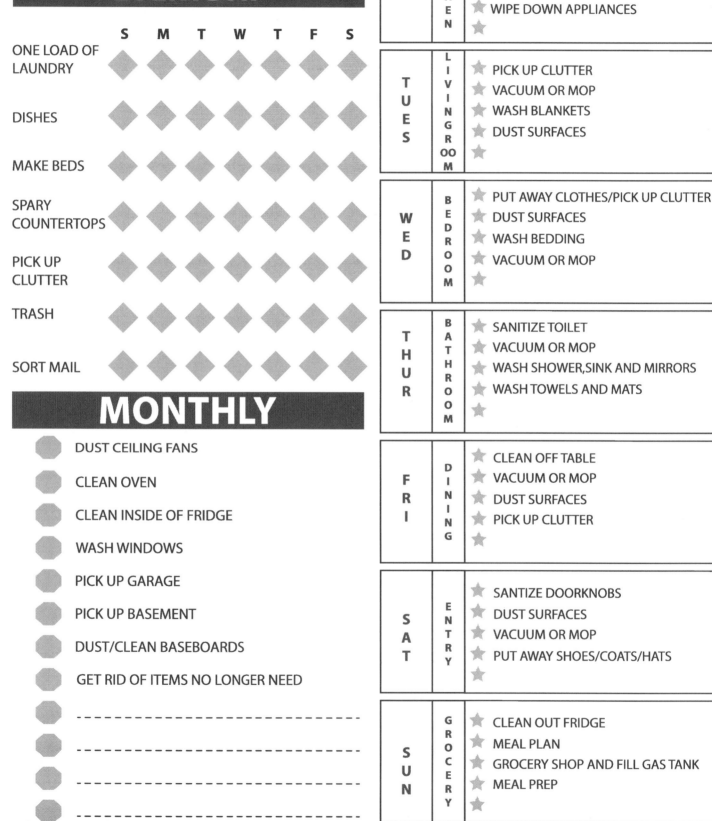

DATE :   CLEANING CHEEKLIST

KEEP A GOOD THING GOING

EVERYDAY

	S	M	T	W	T	F	S
ONE LOAD OF LAUNDRY	◆	◆	◆	◆	◆	◆	◆
DISHES	◆	◆	◆	◆	◆	◆	◆
MAKE BEDS	◆	◆	◆	◆	◆	◆	◆
SPARY COUNTERTOPS	◆	◆	◆	◆	◆	◆	◆
PICK UP CLUTTER	◆	◆	◆	◆	◆	◆	◆
TRASH	◆	◆	◆	◆	◆	◆	◆
SORT MAIL	◆	◆	◆	◆	◆	◆	◆

MONTHLY

- ⬡ DUST CEILING FANS
- ⬡ CLEAN OVEN
- ⬡ CLEAN INSIDE OF FRIDGE
- ⬡ WASH WINDOWS
- ⬡ PICK UP GARAGE
- ⬡ PICK UP BASEMENT
- ⬡ DUST/CLEAN BASEBOARDS
- ⬡ GET RID OF ITEMS NO LONGER NEED
- ⬡ -----------------------------------
- ⬡ -----------------------------------
- ⬡ -----------------------------------
- ⬡

MON — KITCHEN
- ☆ CLEAN KITCHEN TABLE
- ☆ WIPE DOWN SINK AND COUNTERS
- ☆ VACUUM OR MOP
- ☆ WIPE DOWN APPLIANCES
- ☆

TUES — LIVING ROOM
- ☆ PICK UP CLUTTER
- ☆ VACUUM OR MOP
- ☆ WASH BLANKETS
- ☆ DUST SURFACES
- ☆

WED — BEDROOM
- ☆ PUT AWAY CLOTHES/PICK UP CLUTTER
- ☆ DUST SURFACES
- ☆ WASH BEDDING
- ☆ VACUUM OR MOP
- ☆

THUR — BATHROOM
- ☆ SANITIZE TOILET
- ☆ VACUUM OR MOP
- ☆ WASH SHOWER,SINK AND MIRRORS
- ☆ WASH TOWELS AND MATS
- ☆

FRI — DINING
- ☆ CLEAN OFF TABLE
- ☆ VACUUM OR MOP
- ☆ DUST SURFACES
- ☆ PICK UP CLUTTER

SAT — ENTRY
- ☆ SANTIZE DOORKNOBS
- ☆ DUST SURFACES
- ☆ VACUUM OR MOP
- ☆ PUT AWAY SHOES/COATS/HATS
- ☆

SUN — GROCERY
- ☆ CLEAN OUT FRIDGE
- ☆ MEAL PLAN
- ☆ GROCERY SHOP AND FILL GAS TANK
- ☆ MEAL PREP
- ☆

DATE :

CLEANING CHEEKLIST

KEEP A GOOD THING GOING

EVERYDAY

	S	M	T	W	T	F	S
ONE LOAD OF LAUNDRY	◆	◆	◆	◆	◆	◆	◆
DISHES	◆	◆	◆	◆	◆	◆	◆
MAKE BEDS	◆	◆	◆	◆	◆	◆	◆
SPARY COUNTERTOPS	◆	◆	◆	◆	◆	◆	◆
PICK UP CLUTTER	◆	◆	◆	◆	◆	◆	◆
TRASH	◆	◆	◆	◆	◆	◆	◆
SORT MAIL	◆	◆	◆	◆	◆	◆	◆

MONTHLY

- DUST CEILING FANS
- CLEAN OVEN
- CLEAN INSIDE OF FRIDGE
- WASH WINDOWS
- PICK UP GARAGE
- PICK UP BASEMENT
- DUST/CLEAN BASEBOARDS
- GET RID OF ITEMS NO LONGER NEED
- _____
- _____
- _____
- _____

MON	**KITCHEN**	★ CLEAN KITCHEN TABLE ★ WIPE DOWN SINK AND COUNTERS ★ VACUUM OR MOP ★ WIPE DOWN APPLIANCES ★
TUES	**LIVINGROOM**	★ PICK UP CLUTTER ★ VACUUM OR MOP ★ WASH BLANKETS ★ DUST SURFACES ★
WED	**BEDROOM**	★ PUT AWAY CLOTHES/PICK UP CLUTTER ★ DUST SURFACES ★ WASH BEDDING ★ VACUUM OR MOP ★
THUR	**BATHROOM**	★ SANITIZE TOILET ★ VACUUM OR MOP ★ WASH SHOWER,SINK AND MIRRORS ★ WASH TOWELS AND MATS ★
FRI	**DINING**	★ CLEAN OFF TABLE ★ VACUUM OR MOP ★ DUST SURFACES ★ PICK UP CLUTTER ★
SAT	**ENTRY**	★ SANTIZE DOORKNOBS ★ DUST SURFACES ★ VACUUM OR MOP ★ PUT AWAY SHOES/COATS/HATS ★
SUN	**GROCERY**	★ CLEAN OUT FRIDGE ★ MEAL PLAN ★ GROCERY SHOP AND FILL GAS TANK ★ MEAL PREP ★

DATE :

CLEANING CHEEKLIST

KEEP A GOOD THING GOING

EVERYDAY

	S	M	T	W	T	F	S
ONE LOAD OF LAUNDRY	◆	◆	◆	◆	◆	◆	◆
DISHES	◆	◆	◆	◆	◆	◆	◆
MAKE BEDS	◆	◆	◆	◆	◆	◆	◆
SPARY COUNTERTOPS	◆	◆	◆	◆	◆	◆	◆
PICK UP CLUTTER	◆	◆	◆	◆	◆	◆	◆
TRASH	◆	◆	◆	◆	◆	◆	◆
SORT MAIL	◆	◆	◆	◆	◆	◆	◆

MONTHLY

- ⬡ DUST CEILING FANS
- ⬡ CLEAN OVEN
- ⬡ CLEAN INSIDE OF FRIDGE
- ⬡ WASH WINDOWS
- ⬡ PICK UP GARAGE
- ⬡ PICK UP BASEMENT
- ⬡ DUST/CLEAN BASEBOARDS
- ⬡ GET RID OF ITEMS NO LONGER NEED
- ⬡ ------------------------------
- ⬡ ------------------------------
- ⬡ ------------------------------
- ⬡

MON	KITCHEN	☆ CLEAN KITCHEN TABLE ☆ WIPE DOWN SINK AND COUNTERS ☆ VACUUM OR MOP ☆ WIPE DOWN APPLIANCES ☆
TUES	LIVING ROOM	☆ PICK UP CLUTTER ☆ VACUUM OR MOP ☆ WASH BLANKETS ☆ DUST SURFACES ☆
WED	BEDROOM	☆ PUT AWAY CLOTHES/PICK UP CLUTTER ☆ DUST SURFACES ☆ WASH BEDDING ☆ VACUUM OR MOP ☆
THUR	BATHROOM	☆ SANITIZE TOILET ☆ VACUUM OR MOP ☆ WASH SHOWER,SINK AND MIRRORS ☆ WASH TOWELS AND MATS ☆
FRI	DINING	☆ CLEAN OFF TABLE ☆ VACUUM OR MOP ☆ DUST SURFACES ☆ PICK UP CLUTTER ☆
SAT	ENTRY	☆ SANTIZE DOORKNOBS ☆ DUST SURFACES ☆ VACUUM OR MOP ☆ PUT AWAY SHOES/COATS/HATS ☆
SUN	GROCERY	☆ CLEAN OUT FRIDGE ☆ MEAL PLAN ☆ GROCERY SHOP AND FILL GAS TANK ☆ MEAL PREP

DATE :

CLEANING CHEEKLIST

KEEP A GOOD THING GOING

EVERYDAY

	S	M	T	W	T	F	S
ONE LOAD OF LAUNDRY	◆	◆	◆	◆	◆	◆	◆
DISHES	◆	◆	◆	◆	◆	◆	◆
MAKE BEDS	◆	◆	◆	◆	◆	◆	◆
SPARY COUNTERTOPS	◆	◆	◆	◆	◆	◆	◆
PICK UP CLUTTER	◆	◆	◆	◆	◆	◆	◆
TRASH	◆	◆	◆	◆	◆	◆	◆
SORT MAIL	◆	◆	◆	◆	◆	◆	◆

MONTHLY

- DUST CEILING FANS
- CLEAN OVEN
- CLEAN INSIDE OF FRIDGE
- WASH WINDOWS
- PICK UP GARAGE
- PICK UP BASEMENT
- DUST/CLEAN BASEBOARDS
- GET RID OF ITEMS NO LONGER NEED
- -------------------------------
- -------------------------------
- -------------------------------
- -------------------------------

MON — **KITCHEN**
- ★ CLEAN KITCHEN TABLE
- ★ WIPE DOWN SINK AND COUNTERS
- ★ VACUUM OR MOP
- ★ WIPE DOWN APPLIANCES
- ★

TUES — **LIVINGROOM**
- ★ PICK UP CLUTTER
- ★ VACUUM OR MOP
- ★ WASH BLANKETS
- ★ DUST SURFACES
- ★

WED — **BEDROOM**
- ★ PUT AWAY CLOTHES/PICK UP CLUTTER
- ★ DUST SURFACES
- ★ WASH BEDDING
- ★ VACUUM OR MOP
- ★

THUR — **BATHROOM**
- ★ SANITIZE TOILET
- ★ VACUUM OR MOP
- ★ WASH SHOWER,SINK AND MIRRORS
- ★ WASH TOWELS AND MATS
- ★

FRI — **DINING**
- ★ CLEAN OFF TABLE
- ★ VACUUM OR MOP
- ★ DUST SURFACES
- ★ PICK UP CLUTTER

SAT — **ENTRY**
- ★ SANTIZE DOORKNOBS
- ★ DUST SURFACES
- ★ VACUUM OR MOP
- ★ PUT AWAY SHOES/COATS/HATS
- ★

SUN — **GROCERY**
- ★ CLEAN OUT FRIDGE
- ★ MEAL PLAN
- ★ GROCERY SHOP AND FILL GAS TANK
- ★ MEAL PREP
- ★

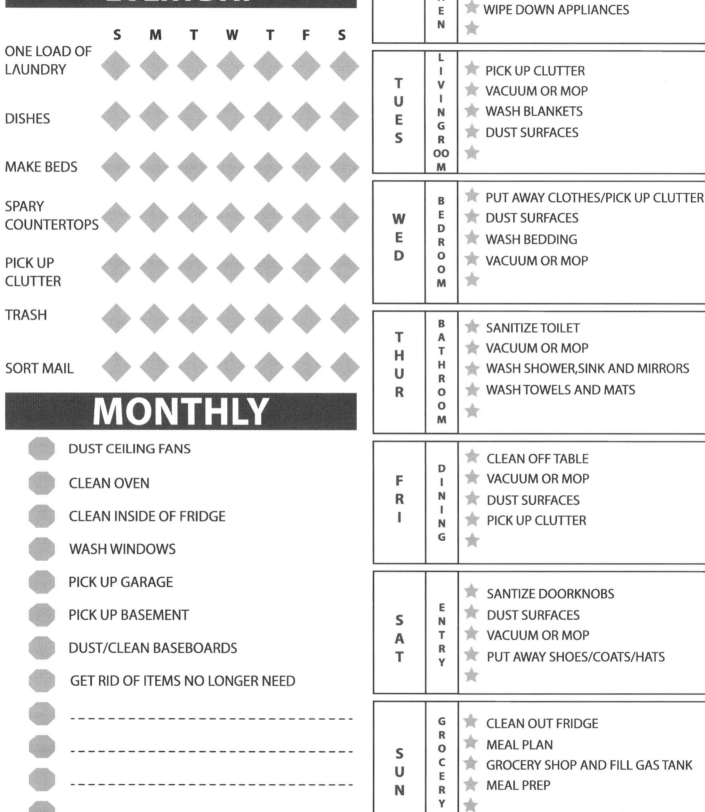

DATE :

CLEANING CHECKLIST

KEEP A GOOD THING GOING

EVERYDAY

	S	M	T	W	T	F	S
ONE LOAD OF LAUNDRY	◆	◆	◆	◆	◆	◆	◆
DISHES	◆	◆	◆	◆	◆	◆	◆
MAKE BEDS	◆	◆	◆	◆	◆	◆	◆
SPARY COUNTERTOPS	◆	◆	◆	◆	◆	◆	◆
PICK UP CLUTTER	◆	◆	◆	◆	◆	◆	◆
TRASH	◆	◆	◆	◆	◆	◆	◆
SORT MAIL	◆	◆	◆	◆	◆	◆	◆

MONTHLY

- DUST CEILING FANS
- CLEAN OVEN
- CLEAN INSIDE OF FRIDGE
- WASH WINDOWS
- PICK UP GARAGE
- PICK UP BASEMENT
- DUST/CLEAN BASEBOARDS
- GET RID OF ITEMS NO LONGER NEED
- ---------------------------------
- ---------------------------------
- ---------------------------------
- ---------------------------------

MON	KITCHEN	★ CLEAN KITCHEN TABLE ★ WIPE DOWN SINK AND COUNTERS ★ VACUUM OR MOP ★ WIPE DOWN APPLIANCES ★
TUES	LIVING ROOM	★ PICK UP CLUTTER ★ VACUUM OR MOP ★ WASH BLANKETS ★ DUST SURFACES ★
WED	BEDROOM	★ PUT AWAY CLOTHES/PICK UP CLUTTER ★ DUST SURFACES ★ WASH BEDDING ★ VACUUM OR MOP ★
THUR	BATHROOM	★ SANITIZE TOILET ★ VACUUM OR MOP ★ WASH SHOWER,SINK AND MIRRORS ★ WASH TOWELS AND MATS ★
FRI	DINING	★ CLEAN OFF TABLE ★ VACUUM OR MOP ★ DUST SURFACES ★ PICK UP CLUTTER ★
SAT	ENTRY	★ SANTIZE DOORKNOBS ★ DUST SURFACES ★ VACUUM OR MOP ★ PUT AWAY SHOES/COATS/HATS ★
SUN	GROCERY	★ CLEAN OUT FRIDGE ★ MEAL PLAN ★ GROCERY SHOP AND FILL GAS TANK ★ MEAL PREP ★

DATE :   CLEANING CHEEKLIST

KEEP A GOOD THING GOING

EVERYDAY

	S	M	T	W	T	F	S
ONE LOAD OF LAUNDRY	◆	◆	◆	◆	◆	◆	◆
DISHES	◆	◆	◆	◆	◆	◆	◆
MAKE BEDS	◆	◆	◆	◆	◆	◆	◆
SPARY COUNTERTOPS	◆	◆	◆	◆	◆	◆	◆
PICK UP CLUTTER	◆	◆	◆	◆	◆	◆	◆
TRASH	◆	◆	◆	◆	◆	◆	◆
SORT MAIL	◆	◆	◆	◆	◆	◆	◆

MONTHLY

- DUST CEILING FANS
- CLEAN OVEN
- CLEAN INSIDE OF FRIDGE
- WASH WINDOWS
- PICK UP GARAGE
- PICK UP BASEMENT
- DUST/CLEAN BASEBOARDS
- GET RID OF ITEMS NO LONGER NEED
- _____
- _____
- _____
- _____

MON — KITCHEN
- ★ CLEAN KITCHEN TABLE
- ★ WIPE DOWN SINK AND COUNTERS
- ★ VACUUM OR MOP
- ★ WIPE DOWN APPLIANCES
- ★

TUES — LIVINGROOM
- ★ PICK UP CLUTTER
- ★ VACUUM OR MOP
- ★ WASH BLANKETS
- ★ DUST SURFACES
- ★

WED — BEDROOM
- ★ PUT AWAY CLOTHES/PICK UP CLUTTER
- ★ DUST SURFACES
- ★ WASH BEDDING
- ★ VACUUM OR MOP
- ★

THUR — BATHROOM
- ★ SANITIZE TOILET
- ★ VACUUM OR MOP
- ★ WASH SHOWER, SINK AND MIRRORS
- ★ WASH TOWELS AND MATS
- ★

FRI — DINING
- ★ CLEAN OFF TABLE
- ★ VACUUM OR MOP
- ★ DUST SURFACES
- ★ PICK UP CLUTTER
- ★

SAT — ENTRY
- ★ SANTIZE DOORKNOBS
- ★ DUST SURFACES
- ★ VACUUM OR MOP
- ★ PUT AWAY SHOES/COATS/HATS
- ★

SUN — GROCERY
- ★ CLEAN OUT FRIDGE
- ★ MEAL PLAN
- ★ GROCERY SHOP AND FILL GAS TANK
- ★ MEAL PREP
- ★

CLEANING CHEEKLIST

KEEP A GOOD THING GOING

EVERYDAY

	S	M	T	W	T	F	S
ONE LOAD OF LAUNDRY	◆	◆	◆	◆	◆	◆	◆
DISHES	◆	◆	◆	◆	◆	◆	◆
MAKE BEDS	◆	◆	◆	◆	◆	◆	◆
SPARY COUNTERTOPS	◆	◆	◆	◆	◆	◆	◆
PICK UP CLUTTER	◆	◆	◆	◆	◆	◆	◆
TRASH	◆	◆	◆	◆	◆	◆	◆
SORT MAIL	◆	◆	◆	◆	◆	◆	◆

MONTHLY

- DUST CEILING FANS
- CLEAN OVEN
- CLEAN INSIDE OF FRIDGE
- WASH WINDOWS
- PICK UP GARAGE
- PICK UP BASEMENT
- DUST/CLEAN BASEBOARDS
- GET RID OF ITEMS NO LONGER NEED
- -
- -
- -
- -

MON	**KITCHEN**	★ CLEAN KITCHEN TABLE ★ WIPE DOWN SINK AND COUNTERS ★ VACUUM OR MOP ★ WIPE DOWN APPLIANCES ★
TUES	**LIVINGROOM**	★ PICK UP CLUTTER ★ VACUUM OR MOP ★ WASH BLANKETS ★ DUST SURFACES ★
WED	**BEDROOM**	★ PUT AWAY CLOTHES/PICK UP CLUTTER ★ DUST SURFACES ★ WASH BEDDING ★ VACUUM OR MOP ★
THUR	**BATHROOM**	★ SANITIZE TOILET ★ VACUUM OR MOP ★ WASH SHOWER,SINK AND MIRRORS ★ WASH TOWELS AND MATS ★
FRI	**DINING**	★ CLEAN OFF TABLE ★ VACUUM OR MOP ★ DUST SURFACES ★ PICK UP CLUTTER ★
SAT	**ENTRY**	★ SANTIZE DOORKNOBS ★ DUST SURFACES ★ VACUUM OR MOP ★ PUT AWAY SHOES/COATS/HATS ★
SUN	**GROCERY**	★ CLEAN OUT FRIDGE ★ MEAL PLAN ★ GROCERY SHOP AND FILL GAS TANK ★ MEAL PREP ★

DATE :

CLEANING CHEEKLIST

KEEP A GOOD THING GOING

EVERYDAY

	S	M	T	W	T	F	S
ONE LOAD OF LAUNDRY	◆	◆	◆	◆	◆	◆	◆
DISHES	◆	◆	◆	◆	◆	◆	◆
MAKE BEDS	◆	◆	◆	◆	◆	◆	◆
SPARY COUNTERTOPS	◆	◆	◆	◆	◆	◆	◆
PICK UP CLUTTER	◆	◆	◆	◆	◆	◆	◆
TRASH	◆	◆	◆	◆	◆	◆	◆
SORT MAIL	◆	◆	◆	◆	◆	◆	◆

MONTHLY

- ⬡ DUST CEILING FANS
- ⬡ CLEAN OVEN
- ⬡ CLEAN INSIDE OF FRIDGE
- ⬡ WASH WINDOWS
- ⬡ PICK UP GARAGE
- ⬡ PICK UP BASEMENT
- ⬡ DUST/CLEAN BASEBOARDS
- ⬡ GET RID OF ITEMS NO LONGER NEED
- ⬡ - - - - - - - - - - - - - - - - - -
- ⬡ - - - - - - - - - - - - - - - - - -
- ⬡ - - - - - - - - - - - - - - - - - -
- ⬡

MON	KITCHEN	★ CLEAN KITCHEN TABLE ★ WIPE DOWN SINK AND COUNTERS ★ VACUUM OR MOP ★ WIPE DOWN APPLIANCES ★
TUES	LIVINGROOM	★ PICK UP CLUTTER ★ VACUUM OR MOP ★ WASH BLANKETS ★ DUST SURFACES ★
WED	BEDROOM	★ PUT AWAY CLOTHES/PICK UP CLUTTER ★ DUST SURFACES ★ WASH BEDDING ★ VACUUM OR MOP ★
THUR	BATHROOM	★ SANITIZE TOILET ★ VACUUM OR MOP ★ WASH SHOWER,SINK AND MIRRORS ★ WASH TOWELS AND MATS ★
FRI	DINING	★ CLEAN OFF TABLE ★ VACUUM OR MOP ★ DUST SURFACES ★ PICK UP CLUTTER ★
SAT	ENTRY	★ SANTIZE DOORKNOBS ★ DUST SURFACES ★ VACUUM OR MOP ★ PUT AWAY SHOES/COATS/HATS ★
SUN	GROCERY	★ CLEAN OUT FRIDGE ★ MEAL PLAN ★ GROCERY SHOP AND FILL GAS TANK ★ MEAL PREP ★

DATE :

CLEANING CHEEKLIST

KEEP A GOOD THING GOING

EVERYDAY

	S	M	T	W	T	F	S
ONE LOAD OF LAUNDRY	◆	◆	◆	◆	◆	◆	◆
DISHES	◆	◆	◆	◆	◆	◆	◆
MAKE BEDS	◆	◆	◆	◆	◆	◆	◆
SPARY COUNTERTOPS	◆	◆	◆	◆	◆	◆	◆
PICK UP CLUTTER	◆	◆	◆	◆	◆	◆	◆
TRASH	◆	◆	◆	◆	◆	◆	◆
SORT MAIL	◆	◆	◆	◆	◆	◆	◆

MONTHLY

- DUST CEILING FANS
- CLEAN OVEN
- CLEAN INSIDE OF FRIDGE
- WASH WINDOWS
- PICK UP GARAGE
- PICK UP BASEMENT
- DUST/CLEAN BASEBOARDS
- GET RID OF ITEMS NO LONGER NEED
- -
- -
- -
- -

MON — KITCHEN
- ★ CLEAN KITCHEN TABLE
- ★ WIPE DOWN SINK AND COUNTERS
- ★ VACUUM OR MOP
- ★ WIPE DOWN APPLIANCES
- ★

TUES — LIVING ROOM
- ★ PICK UP CLUTTER
- ★ VACUUM OR MOP
- ★ WASH BLANKETS
- ★ DUST SURFACES
- ★

WED — BEDROOM
- ★ PUT AWAY CLOTHES/PICK UP CLUTTER
- ★ DUST SURFACES
- ★ WASH BEDDING
- ★ VACUUM OR MOP
- ★

THUR — BATHROOM
- ★ SANITIZE TOILET
- ★ VACUUM OR MOP
- ★ WASH SHOWER,SINK AND MIRRORS
- ★ WASH TOWELS AND MATS
- ★

FRI — DINING
- ★ CLEAN OFF TABLE
- ★ VACUUM OR MOP
- ★ DUST SURFACES
- ★ PICK UP CLUTTER
- ★

SAT — ENTRY
- ★ SANTIZE DOORKNOBS
- ★ DUST SURFACES
- ★ VACUUM OR MOP
- ★ PUT AWAY SHOES/COATS/HATS
- ★

SUN — GROCERY
- ★ CLEAN OUT FRIDGE
- ★ MEAL PLAN
- ★ GROCERY SHOP AND FILL GAS TANK
- ★ MEAL PREP
- ★

DATE :

CLEANING CHEEKLIST

KEEP A GOOD THING GOING

EVERYDAY

	S	M	T	W	T	F	S
ONE LOAD OF LAUNDRY	◆	◆	◆	◆	◆	◆	◆
DISHES	◆	◆	◆	◆	◆	◆	◆
MAKE BEDS	◆	◆	◆	◆	◆	◆	◆
SPARY COUNTERTOPS	◆	◆	◆	◆	◆	◆	◆
PICK UP CLUTTER	◆	◆	◆	◆	◆	◆	◆
TRASH	◆	◆	◆	◆	◆	◆	◆
SORT MAIL	◆	◆	◆	◆	◆	◆	◆

MONTHLY

- DUST CEILING FANS
- CLEAN OVEN
- CLEAN INSIDE OF FRIDGE
- WASH WINDOWS
- PICK UP GARAGE
- PICK UP BASEMENT
- DUST/CLEAN BASEBOARDS
- GET RID OF ITEMS NO LONGER NEED
- -
- -
- -
-

MON	KITCHEN	☆ CLEAN KITCHEN TABLE
		☆ WIPE DOWN SINK AND COUNTERS
		☆ VACUUM OR MOP
		☆ WIPE DOWN APPLIANCES
		☆

TUES	LIVING ROOM	☆ PICK UP CLUTTER
		☆ VACUUM OR MOP
		☆ WASH BLANKETS
		☆ DUST SURFACES
		☆

WED	BEDROOM	☆ PUT AWAY CLOTHES/PICK UP CLUTTER
		☆ DUST SURFACES
		☆ WASH BEDDING
		☆ VACUUM OR MOP
		☆

THUR	BATHROOM	☆ SANITIZE TOILET
		☆ VACUUM OR MOP
		☆ WASH SHOWER,SINK AND MIRRORS
		☆ WASH TOWELS AND MATS
		☆

FRI	DINING	☆ CLEAN OFF TABLE
		☆ VACUUM OR MOP
		☆ DUST SURFACES
		☆ PICK UP CLUTTER
		☆

SAT	ENTRY	☆ SANTIZE DOORKNOBS
		☆ DUST SURFACES
		☆ VACUUM OR MOP
		☆ PUT AWAY SHOES/COATS/HATS
		☆

SUN	GROCERY	☆ CLEAN OUT FRIDGE
		☆ MEAL PLAN
		☆ GROCERY SHOP AND FILL GAS TANK
		☆ MEAL PREP
		☆

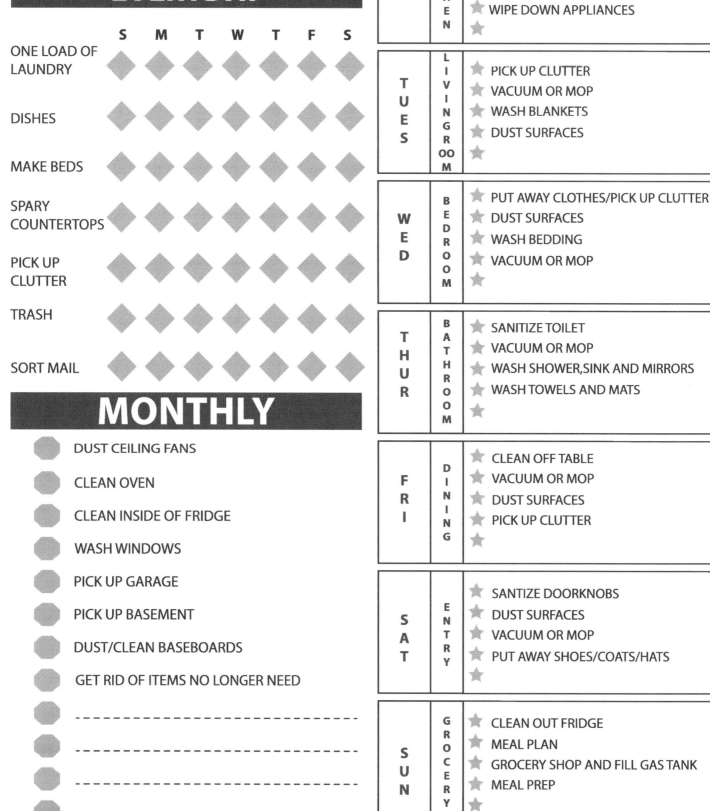

DATE :

CLEANING CHEEKLIST

KEEP A GOOD THING GOING

EVERYDAY

	S	M	T	W	T	F	S
ONE LOAD OF LAUNDRY	◆	◆	◆	◆	◆	◆	◆
DISHES	◆	◆	◆	◆	◆	◆	◆
MAKE BEDS	◆	◆	◆	◆	◆	◆	◆
SPARY COUNTERTOPS	◆	◆	◆	◆	◆	◆	◆
PICK UP CLUTTER	◆	◆	◆	◆	◆	◆	◆
TRASH	◆	◆	◆	◆	◆	◆	◆
SORT MAIL	◆	◆	◆	◆	◆	◆	◆

MONTHLY

- ◯ DUST CEILING FANS
- ◯ CLEAN OVEN
- ◯ CLEAN INSIDE OF FRIDGE
- ◯ WASH WINDOWS
- ◯ PICK UP GARAGE
- ◯ PICK UP BASEMENT
- ◯ DUST/CLEAN BASEBOARDS
- ◯ GET RID OF ITEMS NO LONGER NEED
- ◯ -
- ◯ -
- ◯ -
- ◯ -

MON — KITCHEN
- ★ CLEAN KITCHEN TABLE
- ★ WIPE DOWN SINK AND COUNTERS
- ★ VACUUM OR MOP
- ★ WIPE DOWN APPLIANCES
- ★

TUES — LIVINGROOM
- ★ PICK UP CLUTTER
- ★ VACUUM OR MOP
- ★ WASH BLANKETS
- ★ DUST SURFACES
- ★

WED — BEDROOM
- ★ PUT AWAY CLOTHES/PICK UP CLUTTER
- ★ DUST SURFACES
- ★ WASH BEDDING
- ★ VACUUM OR MOP
- ★

THUR — BATHROOM
- ★ SANITIZE TOILET
- ★ VACUUM OR MOP
- ★ WASH SHOWER,SINK AND MIRRORS
- ★ WASH TOWELS AND MATS
- ★

FRI — DINING
- ★ CLEAN OFF TABLE
- ★ VACUUM OR MOP
- ★ DUST SURFACES
- ★ PICK UP CLUTTER
- ★

SAT — ENTRY
- ★ SANTIZE DOORKNOBS
- ★ DUST SURFACES
- ★ VACUUM OR MOP
- ★ PUT AWAY SHOES/COATS/HATS
- ★

SUN — GROCERY
- ★ CLEAN OUT FRIDGE
- ★ MEAL PLAN
- ★ GROCERY SHOP AND FILL GAS TANK
- ★ MEAL PREP
- ★

DATE : CLEANING CHEEKLIST

KEEP A GOOD THING GOING

EVERYDAY

	S	M	T	W	T	F	S
ONE LOAD OF LAUNDRY	◆	◆	◆	◆	◆	◆	◆
DISHES	◆	◆	◆	◆	◆	◆	◆
MAKE BEDS	◆	◆	◆	◆	◆	◆	◆
SPARY COUNTERTOPS	◆	◆	◆	◆	◆	◆	◆
PICK UP CLUTTER	◆	◆	◆	◆	◆	◆	◆
TRASH	◆	◆	◆	◆	◆	◆	◆
SORT MAIL	◆	◆	◆	◆	◆	◆	◆

MONTHLY

- DUST CEILING FANS
- CLEAN OVEN
- CLEAN INSIDE OF FRIDGE
- WASH WINDOWS
- PICK UP GARAGE
- PICK UP BASEMENT
- DUST/CLEAN BASEBOARDS
- GET RID OF ITEMS NO LONGER NEED
- -
- -
- -
- -

MON — KITCHEN
- ★ CLEAN KITCHEN TABLE
- ★ WIPE DOWN SINK AND COUNTERS
- ★ VACUUM OR MOP
- ★ WIPE DOWN APPLIANCES
- ★

TUES — LIVING ROOM
- ★ PICK UP CLUTTER
- ★ VACUUM OR MOP
- ★ WASH BLANKETS
- ★ DUST SURFACES
- ★

WED — BEDROOM
- ★ PUT AWAY CLOTHES/PICK UP CLUTTER
- ★ DUST SURFACES
- ★ WASH BEDDING
- ★ VACUUM OR MOP
- ★

THUR — BATHROOM
- ★ SANITIZE TOILET
- ★ VACUUM OR MOP
- ★ WASH SHOWER, SINK AND MIRRORS
- ★ WASH TOWELS AND MATS
- ★

FRI — DINING
- ★ CLEAN OFF TABLE
- ★ VACUUM OR MOP
- ★ DUST SURFACES
- ★ PICK UP CLUTTER
- ★

SAT — ENTRY
- ★ SANTIZE DOORKNOBS
- ★ DUST SURFACES
- ★ VACUUM OR MOP
- ★ PUT AWAY SHOES/COATS/HATS
- ★

SUN — GROCERY
- ★ CLEAN OUT FRIDGE
- ★ MEAL PLAN
- ★ GROCERY SHOP AND FILL GAS TANK
- ★ MEAL PREP
- ★

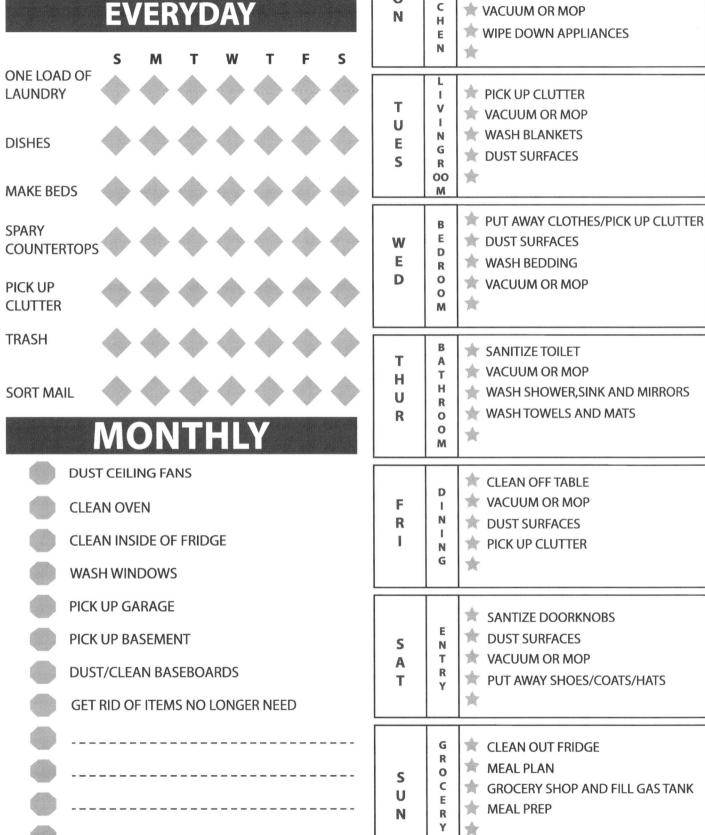

DATE :

CLEANING CHECKLIST

KEEP A GOOD THING GOING

EVERYDAY

	S	M	T	W	T	F	S
ONE LOAD OF LAUNDRY	◈	◈	◈	◈	◈	◈	◈
DISHES	◈	◈	◈	◈	◈	◈	◈
MAKE BEDS	◈	◈	◈	◈	◈	◈	◈
SPARY COUNTERTOPS	◈	◈	◈	◈	◈	◈	◈
PICK UP CLUTTER	◈	◈	◈	◈	◈	◈	◈
TRASH	◈	◈	◈	◈	◈	◈	◈
SORT MAIL	◈	◈	◈	◈	◈	◈	◈

MONTHLY

- DUST CEILING FANS
- CLEAN OVEN
- CLEAN INSIDE OF FRIDGE
- WASH WINDOWS
- PICK UP GARAGE
- PICK UP BASEMENT
- DUST/CLEAN BASEBOARDS
- GET RID OF ITEMS NO LONGER NEED
- _____
- _____
- _____
-

MON — KITCHEN
- ★ CLEAN KITCHEN TABLE
- ★ WIPE DOWN SINK AND COUNTERS
- ★ VACUUM OR MOP
- ★ WIPE DOWN APPLIANCES
- ★

TUES — LIVING ROOM
- ★ PICK UP CLUTTER
- ★ VACUUM OR MOP
- ★ WASH BLANKETS
- ★ DUST SURFACES
- ★

WED — BEDROOM
- ★ PUT AWAY CLOTHES/PICK UP CLUTTER
- ★ DUST SURFACES
- ★ WASH BEDDING
- ★ VACUUM OR MOP
- ★

THUR — BATHROOM
- ★ SANITIZE TOILET
- ★ VACUUM OR MOP
- ★ WASH SHOWER,SINK AND MIRRORS
- ★ WASH TOWELS AND MATS
- ★

FRI — DINING
- ★ CLEAN OFF TABLE
- ★ VACUUM OR MOP
- ★ DUST SURFACES
- ★ PICK UP CLUTTER
- ★

SAT — ENTRY
- ★ SANTIZE DOORKNOBS
- ★ DUST SURFACES
- ★ VACUUM OR MOP
- ★ PUT AWAY SHOES/COATS/HATS
- ★

SUN — GROCERY
- ★ CLEAN OUT FRIDGE
- ★ MEAL PLAN
- ★ GROCERY SHOP AND FILL GAS TANK
- ★ MEAL PREP
- ★

DATE :

CLEANING CHEEKLIST

KEEP A GOOD THING GOING

EVERYDAY

	S	M	T	W	T	F	S
ONE LOAD OF LAUNDRY	◆	◆	◆	◆	◆	◆	◆
DISHES	◆	◆	◆	◆	◆	◆	◆
MAKE BEDS	◆	◆	◆	◆	◆	◆	◆
SPARY COUNTERTOPS	◆	◆	◆	◆	◆	◆	◆
PICK UP CLUTTER	◆	◆	◆	◆	◆	◆	◆
TRASH	◆	◆	◆	◆	◆	◆	◆
SORT MAIL	◆	◆	◆	◆	◆	◆	◆

MONTHLY

- DUST CEILING FANS
- CLEAN OVEN
- CLEAN INSIDE OF FRIDGE
- WASH WINDOWS
- PICK UP GARAGE
- PICK UP BASEMENT
- DUST/CLEAN BASEBOARDS
- GET RID OF ITEMS NO LONGER NEED
- -
- -
- -
- -

MON	KITCHEN	★ CLEAN KITCHEN TABLE ★ WIPE DOWN SINK AND COUNTERS ★ VACUUM OR MOP ★ WIPE DOWN APPLIANCES ★
TUES	LIVINGROOM	★ PICK UP CLUTTER ★ VACUUM OR MOP ★ WASH BLANKETS ★ DUST SURFACES ★
WED	BEDROOM	★ PUT AWAY CLOTHES/PICK UP CLUTTER ★ DUST SURFACES ★ WASH BEDDING ★ VACUUM OR MOP ★
THUR	BATHROOM	★ SANITIZE TOILET ★ VACUUM OR MOP ★ WASH SHOWER,SINK AND MIRRORS ★ WASH TOWELS AND MATS ★
FRI	DINING	★ CLEAN OFF TABLE ★ VACUUM OR MOP ★ DUST SURFACES ★ PICK UP CLUTTER ★
SAT	ENTRY	★ SANTIZE DOORKNOBS ★ DUST SURFACES ★ VACUUM OR MOP ★ PUT AWAY SHOES/COATS/HATS ★
SUN	GROCERY	★ CLEAN OUT FRIDGE ★ MEAL PLAN ★ GROCERY SHOP AND FILL GAS TANK ★ MEAL PREP ★

DATE :

CLEANING CHEEKLIST

KEEP A GOOD THING GOING

EVERYDAY

	S	M	T	W	T	F	S
ONE LOAD OF LAUNDRY	◆	◆	◆	◆	◆	◆	◆
DISHES	◆	◆	◆	◆	◆	◆	◆
MAKE BEDS	◆	◆	◆	◆	◆	◆	◆
SPARY COUNTERTOPS	◆	◆	◆	◆	◆	◆	◆
PICK UP CLUTTER	◆	◆	◆	◆	◆	◆	◆
TRASH	◆	◆	◆	◆	◆	◆	◆
SORT MAIL	◆	◆	◆	◆	◆	◆	◆

MONTHLY

- DUST CEILING FANS
- CLEAN OVEN
- CLEAN INSIDE OF FRIDGE
- WASH WINDOWS
- PICK UP GARAGE
- PICK UP BASEMENT
- DUST/CLEAN BASEBOARDS
- GET RID OF ITEMS NO LONGER NEED
- ------------------------------
- ------------------------------
- ------------------------------

MON — KITCHEN
- ★ CLEAN KITCHEN TABLE
- ★ WIPE DOWN SINK AND COUNTERS
- ★ VACUUM OR MOP
- ★ WIPE DOWN APPLIANCES
- ★

TUES — LIVING ROOM
- ★ PICK UP CLUTTER
- ★ VACUUM OR MOP
- ★ WASH BLANKETS
- ★ DUST SURFACES
- ★

WED — BEDROOM
- ★ PUT AWAY CLOTHES/PICK UP CLUTTER
- ★ DUST SURFACES
- ★ WASH BEDDING
- ★ VACUUM OR MOP
- ★

THUR — BATHROOM
- ★ SANITIZE TOILET
- ★ VACUUM OR MOP
- ★ WASH SHOWER,SINK AND MIRRORS
- ★ WASH TOWELS AND MATS
- ★

FRI — DINING
- ★ CLEAN OFF TABLE
- ★ VACUUM OR MOP
- ★ DUST SURFACES
- ★ PICK UP CLUTTER
- ★

SAT — ENTRY
- ★ SANTIZE DOORKNOBS
- ★ DUST SURFACES
- ★ VACUUM OR MOP
- ★ PUT AWAY SHOES/COATS/HATS
- ★

SUN — GROCERY
- ★ CLEAN OUT FRIDGE
- ★ MEAL PLAN
- ★ GROCERY SHOP AND FILL GAS TANK
- ★ MEAL PREP
- ★

DATE :

CLEANING CHEEKLIST

KEEP A GOOD THING GOING

EVERYDAY

	S	M	T	W	T	F	S
ONE LOAD OF LAUNDRY	◆	◆	◆	◆	◆	◆	◆
DISHES	◆	◆	◆	◆	◆	◆	◆
MAKE BEDS	◆	◆	◆	◆	◆	◆	◆
SPARY COUNTERTOPS	◆	◆	◆	◆	◆	◆	◆
PICK UP CLUTTER	◆	◆	◆	◆	◆	◆	◆
TRASH	◆	◆	◆	◆	◆	◆	◆
SORT MAIL	◆	◆	◆	◆	◆	◆	◆

MONTHLY

- ⬡ DUST CEILING FANS
- ⬡ CLEAN OVEN
- ⬡ CLEAN INSIDE OF FRIDGE
- ⬡ WASH WINDOWS
- ⬡ PICK UP GARAGE
- ⬡ PICK UP BASEMENT
- ⬡ DUST/CLEAN BASEBOARDS
- ⬡ GET RID OF ITEMS NO LONGER NEED
- ⬡ _____
- ⬡ _____
- ⬡ _____
- ⬡ _____

Day	Room	Tasks
MON	**KITCHEN**	★ CLEAN KITCHEN TABLE ★ WIPE DOWN SINK AND COUNTERS ★ VACUUM OR MOP ★ WIPE DOWN APPLIANCES ★
TUES	**LIVINGROOM**	★ PICK UP CLUTTER ★ VACUUM OR MOP ★ WASH BLANKETS ★ DUST SURFACES ★
WED	**BEDROOM**	★ PUT AWAY CLOTHES/PICK UP CLUTTER ★ DUST SURFACES ★ WASH BEDDING ★ VACUUM OR MOP ★
THUR	**BATHROOM**	★ SANITIZE TOILET ★ VACUUM OR MOP ★ WASH SHOWER,SINK AND MIRRORS ★ WASH TOWELS AND MATS ★
FRI	**DINING**	★ CLEAN OFF TABLE ★ VACUUM OR MOP ★ DUST SURFACES ★ PICK UP CLUTTER ★
SAT	**ENTRY**	★ SANTIZE DOORKNOBS ★ DUST SURFACES ★ VACUUM OR MOP ★ PUT AWAY SHOES/COATS/HATS ★
SUN	**GROCERY**	★ CLEAN OUT FRIDGE ★ MEAL PLAN ★ GROCERY SHOP AND FILL GAS TANK ★ MEAL PREP ★

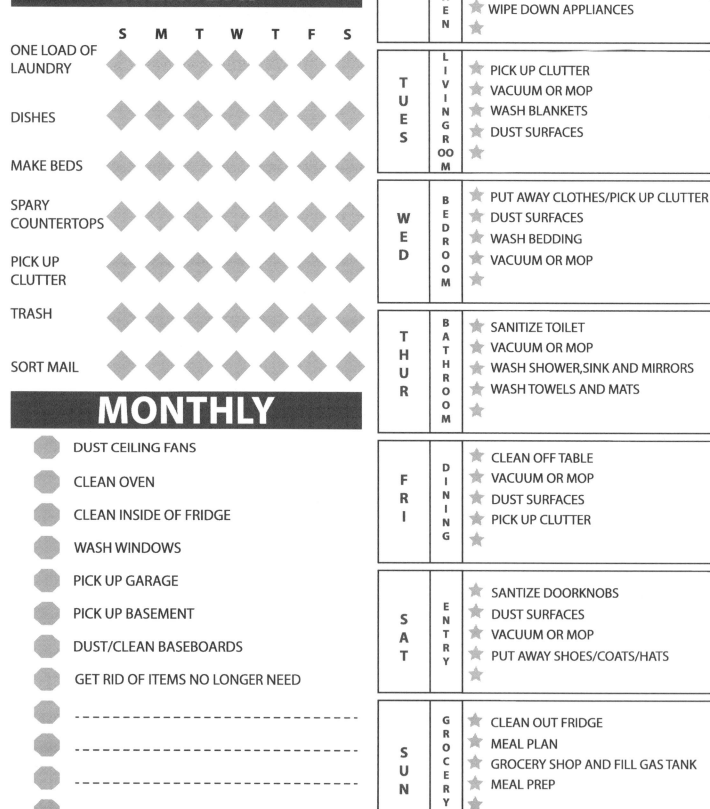

DATE :

CLEANING CHEEKLIST

KEEP A GOOD THING GOING

EVERYDAY

	S	M	T	W	T	F	S
ONE LOAD OF LAUNDRY	◆	◆	◆	◆	◆	◆	◆
DISHES	◆	◆	◆	◆	◆	◆	◆
MAKE BEDS	◆	◆	◆	◆	◆	◆	◆
SPARY COUNTERTOPS	◆	◆	◆	◆	◆	◆	◆
PICK UP CLUTTER	◆	◆	◆	◆	◆	◆	◆
TRASH	◆	◆	◆	◆	◆	◆	◆
SORT MAIL	◆	◆	◆	◆	◆	◆	◆

MONTHLY

- DUST CEILING FANS
- CLEAN OVEN
- CLEAN INSIDE OF FRIDGE
- WASH WINDOWS
- PICK UP GARAGE
- PICK UP BASEMENT
- DUST/CLEAN BASEBOARDS
- GET RID OF ITEMS NO LONGER NEED
- ------------------------------
- ------------------------------
- ------------------------------
- ------------------------------

MON	KITCHEN	☆ CLEAN KITCHEN TABLE
		☆ WIPE DOWN SINK AND COUNTERS
		☆ VACUUM OR MOP
		☆ WIPE DOWN APPLIANCES
		☆

TUES	LIVINGROOM	☆ PICK UP CLUTTER
		☆ VACUUM OR MOP
		☆ WASH BLANKETS
		☆ DUST SURFACES
		☆

WED	BEDROOM	☆ PUT AWAY CLOTHES/PICK UP CLUTTER
		☆ DUST SURFACES
		☆ WASH BEDDING
		☆ VACUUM OR MOP
		☆

THUR	BATHROOM	☆ SANITIZE TOILET
		☆ VACUUM OR MOP
		☆ WASH SHOWER,SINK AND MIRRORS
		☆ WASH TOWELS AND MATS
		☆

FRI	DINING	☆ CLEAN OFF TABLE
		☆ VACUUM OR MOP
		☆ DUST SURFACES
		☆ PICK UP CLUTTER
		☆

SAT	ENTRY	☆ SANTIZE DOORKNOBS
		☆ DUST SURFACES
		☆ VACUUM OR MOP
		☆ PUT AWAY SHOES/COATS/HATS
		☆

SUN	GROCERY	☆ CLEAN OUT FRIDGE
		☆ MEAL PLAN
		☆ GROCERY SHOP AND FILL GAS TANK
		☆ MEAL PREP

DATE :

CLEANING CHEEKLIST

KEEP A GOOD THING GOING

EVERYDAY

	S	M	T	W	T	F	S
ONE LOAD OF LAUNDRY	◆	◆	◆	◆	◆	◆	◆
DISHES	◆	◆	◆	◆	◆	◆	◆
MAKE BEDS	◆	◆	◆	◆	◆	◆	◆
SPARY COUNTERTOPS	◆	◆	◆	◆	◆	◆	◆
PICK UP CLUTTER	◆	◆	◆	◆	◆	◆	◆
TRASH	◆	◆	◆	◆	◆	◆	◆
SORT MAIL	◆	◆	◆	◆	◆	◆	◆

MONTHLY

- DUST CEILING FANS
- CLEAN OVEN
- CLEAN INSIDE OF FRIDGE
- WASH WINDOWS
- PICK UP GARAGE
- PICK UP BASEMENT
- DUST/CLEAN BASEBOARDS
- GET RID OF ITEMS NO LONGER NEED
- ------------------------------
- ------------------------------
- ------------------------------
-

MON	KITCHEN	★ CLEAN KITCHEN TABLE ★ WIPE DOWN SINK AND COUNTERS ★ VACUUM OR MOP ★ WIPE DOWN APPLIANCES ★
TUES	LIVINGROOM	★ PICK UP CLUTTER ★ VACUUM OR MOP ★ WASH BLANKETS ★ DUST SURFACES ★
WED	BEDROOM	★ PUT AWAY CLOTHES/PICK UP CLUTTER ★ DUST SURFACES ★ WASH BEDDING ★ VACUUM OR MOP ★
THUR	BATHROOM	★ SANITIZE TOILET ★ VACUUM OR MOP ★ WASH SHOWER,SINK AND MIRRORS ★ WASH TOWELS AND MATS ★
FRI	DINING	★ CLEAN OFF TABLE ★ VACUUM OR MOP ★ DUST SURFACES ★ PICK UP CLUTTER ★
SAT	ENTRY	★ SANTIZE DOORKNOBS ★ DUST SURFACES ★ VACUUM OR MOP ★ PUT AWAY SHOES/COATS/HATS ★
SUN	GROCERY	★ CLEAN OUT FRIDGE ★ MEAL PLAN ★ GROCERY SHOP AND FILL GAS TANK ★ MEAL PREP ★

DATE :

CLEANING CHEEKLIST

KEEP A GOOD THING GOING

EVERYDAY

	S	M	T	W	T	F	S
ONE LOAD OF LAUNDRY	◆	◆	◆	◆	◆	◆	◆
DISHES	◆	◆	◆	◆	◆	◆	◆
MAKE BEDS	◆	◆	◆	◆	◆	◆	◆
SPARY COUNTERTOPS	◆	◆	◆	◆	◆	◆	◆
PICK UP CLUTTER	◆	◆	◆	◆	◆	◆	◆
TRASH	◆	◆	◆	◆	◆	◆	◆
SORT MAIL	◆	◆	◆	◆	◆	◆	◆

MONTHLY

- DUST CEILING FANS
- CLEAN OVEN
- CLEAN INSIDE OF FRIDGE
- WASH WINDOWS
- PICK UP GARAGE
- PICK UP BASEMENT
- DUST/CLEAN BASEBOARDS
- GET RID OF ITEMS NO LONGER NEED
- ---------------------------------
- ---------------------------------
- ---------------------------------
-

MON — KITCHEN
- ★ CLEAN KITCHEN TABLE
- ★ WIPE DOWN SINK AND COUNTERS
- ★ VACUUM OR MOP
- ★ WIPE DOWN APPLIANCES
- ★

TUES — LIVINGROOM
- ★ PICK UP CLUTTER
- ★ VACUUM OR MOP
- ★ WASH BLANKETS
- ★ DUST SURFACES
- ★

WED — BEDROOM
- ★ PUT AWAY CLOTHES/PICK UP CLUTTER
- ★ DUST SURFACES
- ★ WASH BEDDING
- ★ VACUUM OR MOP
- ★

THUR — BATHROOM
- ★ SANITIZE TOILET
- ★ VACUUM OR MOP
- ★ WASH SHOWER,SINK AND MIRRORS
- ★ WASH TOWELS AND MATS
- ★

FRI — DINING
- ★ CLEAN OFF TABLE
- ★ VACUUM OR MOP
- ★ DUST SURFACES
- ★ PICK UP CLUTTER
- ★

SAT — ENTRY
- ★ SANTIZE DOORKNOBS
- ★ DUST SURFACES
- ★ VACUUM OR MOP
- ★ PUT AWAY SHOES/COATS/HATS
- ★

SUN — GROCERY
- ★ CLEAN OUT FRIDGE
- ★ MEAL PLAN
- ★ GROCERY SHOP AND FILL GAS TANK
- ★ MEAL PREP

DATE :

CLEANING CHEEKLIST

KEEP A GOOD THING GOING

EVERYDAY

	S	M	T	W	T	F	S
ONE LOAD OF LAUNDRY	◆	◆	◆	◆	◆	◆	◆
DISHES	◆	◆	◆	◆	◆	◆	◆
MAKE BEDS	◆	◆	◆	◆	◆	◆	◆
SPARY COUNTERTOPS	◆	◆	◆	◆	◆	◆	◆
PICK UP CLUTTER	◆	◆	◆	◆	◆	◆	◆
TRASH	◆	◆	◆	◆	◆	◆	◆
SORT MAIL	◆	◆	◆	◆	◆	◆	◆

MONTHLY

- ⬡ DUST CEILING FANS
- ⬡ CLEAN OVEN
- ⬡ CLEAN INSIDE OF FRIDGE
- ⬡ WASH WINDOWS
- ⬡ PICK UP GARAGE
- ⬡ PICK UP BASEMENT
- ⬡ DUST/CLEAN BASEBOARDS
- ⬡ GET RID OF ITEMS NO LONGER NEED
- ⬡ -
- ⬡ -
- ⬡ -
- ⬡

MON — KITCHEN
- ★ CLEAN KITCHEN TABLE
- ★ WIPE DOWN SINK AND COUNTERS
- ★ VACUUM OR MOP
- ★ WIPE DOWN APPLIANCES
- ★

TUES — LIVINGROOM
- ★ PICK UP CLUTTER
- ★ VACUUM OR MOP
- ★ WASH BLANKETS
- ★ DUST SURFACES
- ★

WED — BEDROOM
- ★ PUT AWAY CLOTHES/PICK UP CLUTTER
- ★ DUST SURFACES
- ★ WASH BEDDING
- ★ VACUUM OR MOP
- ★

THUR — BATHROOM
- ★ SANITIZE TOILET
- ★ VACUUM OR MOP
- ★ WASH SHOWER,SINK AND MIRRORS
- ★ WASH TOWELS AND MATS
- ★

FRI — DINING
- ★ CLEAN OFF TABLE
- ★ VACUUM OR MOP
- ★ DUST SURFACES
- ★ PICK UP CLUTTER
- ★

SAT — ENTRY
- ★ SANTIZE DOORKNOBS
- ★ DUST SURFACES
- ★ VACUUM OR MOP
- ★ PUT AWAY SHOES/COATS/HATS
- ★

SUN — GROCERY
- ★ CLEAN OUT FRIDGE
- ★ MEAL PLAN
- ★ GROCERY SHOP AND FILL GAS TANK
- ★ MEAL PREP
- ★

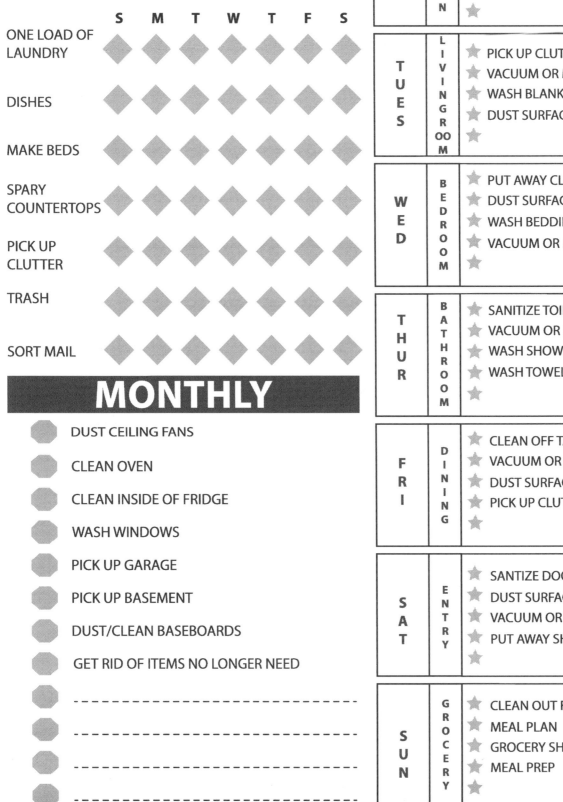

DATE :

CLEANING CHEEKLIST

KEEP A GOOD THING GOING

EVERYDAY

	S	M	T	W	T	F	S
ONE LOAD OF LAUNDRY	◆	◆	◆	◆	◆	◆	◆
DISHES	◆	◆	◆	◆	◆	◆	◆
MAKE BEDS	◆	◆	◆	◆	◆	◆	◆
SPARY COUNTERTOPS	◆	◆	◆	◆	◆	◆	◆
PICK UP CLUTTER	◆	◆	◆	◆	◆	◆	◆
TRASH	◆	◆	◆	◆	◆	◆	◆
SORT MAIL	◆	◆	◆	◆	◆	◆	◆

MONTHLY

- DUST CEILING FANS
- CLEAN OVEN
- CLEAN INSIDE OF FRIDGE
- WASH WINDOWS
- PICK UP GARAGE
- PICK UP BASEMENT
- DUST/CLEAN BASEBOARDS
- GET RID OF ITEMS NO LONGER NEED
- _____
- _____
- _____

MON — KITCHEN
- ☆ CLEAN KITCHEN TABLE
- ☆ WIPE DOWN SINK AND COUNTERS
- ☆ VACUUM OR MOP
- ☆ WIPE DOWN APPLIANCES
- ☆

TUES — LIVINGROOM
- ☆ PICK UP CLUTTER
- ☆ VACUUM OR MOP
- ☆ WASH BLANKETS
- ☆ DUST SURFACES
- ☆

WED — BEDROOM
- ☆ PUT AWAY CLOTHES/PICK UP CLUTTER
- ☆ DUST SURFACES
- ☆ WASH BEDDING
- ☆ VACUUM OR MOP
- ☆

THUR — BATHROOM
- ☆ SANITIZE TOILET
- ☆ VACUUM OR MOP
- ☆ WASH SHOWER, SINK AND MIRRORS
- ☆ WASH TOWELS AND MATS
- ☆

FRI — DINING
- ☆ CLEAN OFF TABLE
- ☆ VACUUM OR MOP
- ☆ DUST SURFACES
- ☆ PICK UP CLUTTER

SAT — ENTRY
- ☆ SANTIZE DOORKNOBS
- ☆ DUST SURFACES
- ☆ VACUUM OR MOP
- ☆ PUT AWAY SHOES/COATS/HATS
- ☆

SUN — GROCERY
- ☆ CLEAN OUT FRIDGE
- ☆ MEAL PLAN
- ☆ GROCERY SHOP AND FILL GAS TANK
- ☆ MEAL PREP

DATE :

CLEANING CHEEKLIST

KEEP A GOOD THING GOING

EVERYDAY

	S	M	T	W	T	F	S
ONE LOAD OF LAUNDRY	◆	◆	◆	◆	◆	◆	◆
DISHES	◆	◆	◆	◆	◆	◆	◆
MAKE BEDS	◆	◆	◆	◆	◆	◆	◆
SPARY COUNTERTOPS	◆	◆	◆	◆	◆	◆	◆
PICK UP CLUTTER	◆	◆	◆	◆	◆	◆	◆
TRASH	◆	◆	◆	◆	◆	◆	◆
SORT MAIL	◆	◆	◆	◆	◆	◆	◆

MONTHLY

- DUST CEILING FANS
- CLEAN OVEN
- CLEAN INSIDE OF FRIDGE
- WASH WINDOWS
- PICK UP GARAGE
- PICK UP BASEMENT
- DUST/CLEAN BASEBOARDS
- GET RID OF ITEMS NO LONGER NEED
- ------------------------------
- ------------------------------
- ------------------------------
-

MON	KITCHEN	★ CLEAN KITCHEN TABLE ★ WIPE DOWN SINK AND COUNTERS ★ VACUUM OR MOP ★ WIPE DOWN APPLIANCES ★
TUES	LIVING ROOM	★ PICK UP CLUTTER ★ VACUUM OR MOP ★ WASH BLANKETS ★ DUST SURFACES ★
WED	BEDROOM	★ PUT AWAY CLOTHES/PICK UP CLUTTER ★ DUST SURFACES ★ WASH BEDDING ★ VACUUM OR MOP ★
THUR	BATHROOM	★ SANITIZE TOILET ★ VACUUM OR MOP ★ WASH SHOWER,SINK AND MIRRORS ★ WASH TOWELS AND MATS ★
FRI	DINING	★ CLEAN OFF TABLE ★ VACUUM OR MOP ★ DUST SURFACES ★ PICK UP CLUTTER
SAT	ENTRY	★ SANTIZE DOORKNOBS ★ DUST SURFACES ★ VACUUM OR MOP ★ PUT AWAY SHOES/COATS/HATS ★
SUN	GROCERY	★ CLEAN OUT FRIDGE ★ MEAL PLAN ★ GROCERY SHOP AND FILL GAS TANK ★ MEAL PREP ★

DATE:

CLEANING CHEEKLIST

KEEP A GOOD THING GOING

EVERYDAY

	S	M	T	W	T	F	S
ONE LOAD OF LAUNDRY	◆	◆	◆	◆	◆	◆	◆
DISHES	◆	◆	◆	◆	◆	◆	◆
MAKE BEDS	◆	◆	◆	◆	◆	◆	◆
SPARY COUNTERTOPS	◆	◆	◆	◆	◆	◆	◆
PICK UP CLUTTER	◆	◆	◆	◆	◆	◆	◆
TRASH	◆	◆	◆	◆	◆	◆	◆
SORT MAIL	◆	◆	◆	◆	◆	◆	◆

MONTHLY

- DUST CEILING FANS
- CLEAN OVEN
- CLEAN INSIDE OF FRIDGE
- WASH WINDOWS
- PICK UP GARAGE
- PICK UP BASEMENT
- DUST/CLEAN BASEBOARDS
- GET RID OF ITEMS NO LONGER NEED
- -
- -
- -

MON — KITCHEN
- ★ CLEAN KITCHEN TABLE
- ★ WIPE DOWN SINK AND COUNTERS
- ★ VACUUM OR MOP
- ★ WIPE DOWN APPLIANCES
- ★

TUES — LIVINGROOM
- ★ PICK UP CLUTTER
- ★ VACUUM OR MOP
- ★ WASH BLANKETS
- ★ DUST SURFACES
- ★

WED — BEDROOM
- ★ PUT AWAY CLOTHES/PICK UP CLUTTER
- ★ DUST SURFACES
- ★ WASH BEDDING
- ★ VACUUM OR MOP
- ★

THUR — BATHROOM
- ★ SANITIZE TOILET
- ★ VACUUM OR MOP
- ★ WASH SHOWER, SINK AND MIRRORS
- ★ WASH TOWELS AND MATS
- ★

FRI — DINING
- ★ CLEAN OFF TABLE
- ★ VACUUM OR MOP
- ★ DUST SURFACES
- ★ PICK UP CLUTTER
- ★

SAT — ENTRY
- ★ SANTIZE DOORKNOBS
- ★ DUST SURFACES
- ★ VACUUM OR MOP
- ★ PUT AWAY SHOES/COATS/HATS
- ★

SUN — GROCERY
- ★ CLEAN OUT FRIDGE
- ★ MEAL PLAN
- ★ GROCERY SHOP AND FILL GAS TANK
- ★ MEAL PREP
- ★

DATE :

CLEANING CHEEKLIST

KEEP A GOOD THING GOING

EVERYDAY

	S	M	T	W	T	F	S
ONE LOAD OF LAUNDRY	◆	◆	◆	◆	◆	◆	◆
DISHES	◆	◆	◆	◆	◆	◆	◆
MAKE BEDS	◆	◆	◆	◆	◆	◆	◆
SPARY COUNTERTOPS	◆	◆	◆	◆	◆	◆	◆
PICK UP CLUTTER	◆	◆	◆	◆	◆	◆	◆
TRASH	◆	◆	◆	◆	◆	◆	◆
SORT MAIL	◆	◆	◆	◆	◆	◆	◆

MONTHLY

- ⬡ DUST CEILING FANS
- ⬡ CLEAN OVEN
- ⬡ CLEAN INSIDE OF FRIDGE
- ⬡ WASH WINDOWS
- ⬡ PICK UP GARAGE
- ⬡ PICK UP BASEMENT
- ⬡ DUST/CLEAN BASEBOARDS
- ⬡ GET RID OF ITEMS NO LONGER NEED
- ⬡ -----------------------------
- ⬡ -----------------------------
- ⬡ -----------------------------
- ⬡ -----------------------------

MON	KITCHEN	★ CLEAN KITCHEN TABLE ★ WIPE DOWN SINK AND COUNTERS ★ VACUUM OR MOP ★ WIPE DOWN APPLIANCES ★
TUES	LIVINGROOM	★ PICK UP CLUTTER ★ VACUUM OR MOP ★ WASH BLANKETS ★ DUST SURFACES ★
WED	BEDROOM	★ PUT AWAY CLOTHES/PICK UP CLUTTER ★ DUST SURFACES ★ WASH BEDDING ★ VACUUM OR MOP ★
THUR	BATHROOM	★ SANITIZE TOILET ★ VACUUM OR MOP ★ WASH SHOWER,SINK AND MIRRORS ★ WASH TOWELS AND MATS ★
FRI	DINING	★ CLEAN OFF TABLE ★ VACUUM OR MOP ★ DUST SURFACES ★ PICK UP CLUTTER ★
SAT	ENTRY	★ SANTIZE DOORKNOBS ★ DUST SURFACES ★ VACUUM OR MOP ★ PUT AWAY SHOES/COATS/HATS ★
SUN	GROCERY	★ CLEAN OUT FRIDGE ★ MEAL PLAN ★ GROCERY SHOP AND FILL GAS TANK ★ MEAL PREP ★

DATE :

CLEANING CHEEKLIST

KEEP A GOOD THING GOING

EVERYDAY

	S	M	T	W	T	F	S
ONE LOAD OF LAUNDRY	◆	◆	◆	◆	◆	◆	◆
DISHES	◆	◆	◆	◆	◆	◆	◆
MAKE BEDS	◆	◆	◆	◆	◆	◆	◆
SPARY COUNTERTOPS	◆	◆	◆	◆	◆	◆	◆
PICK UP CLUTTER	◆	◆	◆	◆	◆	◆	◆
TRASH	◆	◆	◆	◆	◆	◆	◆
SORT MAIL	◆	◆	◆	◆	◆	◆	◆

MONTHLY

- ⬡ DUST CEILING FANS
- ⬡ CLEAN OVEN
- ⬡ CLEAN INSIDE OF FRIDGE
- ⬡ WASH WINDOWS
- ⬡ PICK UP GARAGE
- ⬡ PICK UP BASEMENT
- ⬡ DUST/CLEAN BASEBOARDS
- ⬡ GET RID OF ITEMS NO LONGER NEED
- ⬡ -
- ⬡ -
- ⬡ -
- ⬡

MON — **KITCHEN**
- ★ CLEAN KITCHEN TABLE
- ★ WIPE DOWN SINK AND COUNTERS
- ★ VACUUM OR MOP
- ★ WIPE DOWN APPLIANCES
- ★

TUES — **LIVING ROOM**
- ★ PICK UP CLUTTER
- ★ VACUUM OR MOP
- ★ WASH BLANKETS
- ★ DUST SURFACES
- ★

WED — **BEDROOM**
- ★ PUT AWAY CLOTHES/PICK UP CLUTTER
- ★ DUST SURFACES
- ★ WASH BEDDING
- ★ VACUUM OR MOP
- ★

THUR — **BATHROOM**
- ★ SANITIZE TOILET
- ★ VACUUM OR MOP
- ★ WASH SHOWER,SINK AND MIRRORS
- ★ WASH TOWELS AND MATS
- ★

FRI — **DINING**
- ★ CLEAN OFF TABLE
- ★ VACUUM OR MOP
- ★ DUST SURFACES
- ★ PICK UP CLUTTER
- ★

SAT — **ENTRY**
- ★ SANTIZE DOORKNOBS
- ★ DUST SURFACES
- ★ VACUUM OR MOP
- ★ PUT AWAY SHOES/COATS/HATS
- ★

SUN — **GROCERY**
- ★ CLEAN OUT FRIDGE
- ★ MEAL PLAN
- ★ GROCERY SHOP AND FILL GAS TANK
- ★ MEAL PREP

DATE :

CLEANING CHEEKLIST

KEEP A GOOD THING GOING

EVERYDAY

	S	M	T	W	T	F	S
ONE LOAD OF LAUNDRY	◆	◆	◆	◆	◆	◆	◆
DISHES	◆	◆	◆	◆	◆	◆	◆
MAKE BEDS	◆	◆	◆	◆	◆	◆	◆
SPARY COUNTERTOPS	◆	◆	◆	◆	◆	◆	◆
PICK UP CLUTTER	◆	◆	◆	◆	◆	◆	◆
TRASH	◆	◆	◆	◆	◆	◆	◆
SORT MAIL	◆	◆	◆	◆	◆	◆	◆

MONTHLY

- ⬡ DUST CEILING FANS
- ⬡ CLEAN OVEN
- ⬡ CLEAN INSIDE OF FRIDGE
- ⬡ WASH WINDOWS
- ⬡ PICK UP GARAGE
- ⬡ PICK UP BASEMENT
- ⬡ DUST/CLEAN BASEBOARDS
- ⬡ GET RID OF ITEMS NO LONGER NEED
- ⬡ ------------------------------
- ⬡ ------------------------------
- ⬡ ------------------------------
- ⬡

MON — KITCHEN
- ★ CLEAN KITCHEN TABLE
- ★ WIPE DOWN SINK AND COUNTERS
- ★ VACUUM OR MOP
- ★ WIPE DOWN APPLIANCES
- ★

TUES — LIVINGROOM
- ★ PICK UP CLUTTER
- ★ VACUUM OR MOP
- ★ WASH BLANKETS
- ★ DUST SURFACES
- ★

WED — BEDROOM
- ★ PUT AWAY CLOTHES/PICK UP CLUTTER
- ★ DUST SURFACES
- ★ WASH BEDDING
- ★ VACUUM OR MOP
- ★

THUR — BATHROOM
- ★ SANITIZE TOILET
- ★ VACUUM OR MOP
- ★ WASH SHOWER,SINK AND MIRRORS
- ★ WASH TOWELS AND MATS
- ★

FRI — DINING
- ★ CLEAN OFF TABLE
- ★ VACUUM OR MOP
- ★ DUST SURFACES
- ★ PICK UP CLUTTER
- ★

SAT — ENTRY
- ★ SANTIZE DOORKNOBS
- ★ DUST SURFACES
- ★ VACUUM OR MOP
- ★ PUT AWAY SHOES/COATS/HATS
- ★

SUN — GROCERY
- ★ CLEAN OUT FRIDGE
- ★ MEAL PLAN
- ★ GROCERY SHOP AND FILL GAS TANK
- ★ MEAL PREP
- ★

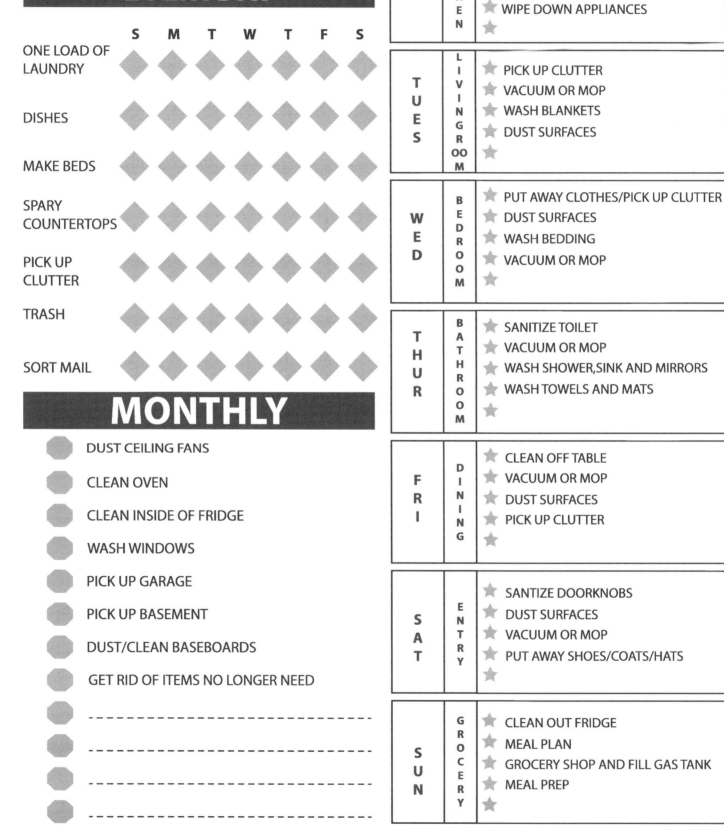

DATE :

CLEANING CHEEKLIST

KEEP A GOOD THING GOING

EVERYDAY

	S	M	T	W	T	F	S
ONE LOAD OF LAUNDRY	◆	◆	◆	◆	◆	◆	◆
DISHES	◆	◆	◆	◆	◆	◆	◆
MAKE BEDS	◆	◆	◆	◆	◆	◆	◆
SPARY COUNTERTOPS	◆	◆	◆	◆	◆	◆	◆
PICK UP CLUTTER	◆	◆	◆	◆	◆	◆	◆
TRASH	◆	◆	◆	◆	◆	◆	◆
SORT MAIL	◆	◆	◆	◆	◆	◆	◆

MONTHLY

- DUST CEILING FANS
- CLEAN OVEN
- CLEAN INSIDE OF FRIDGE
- WASH WINDOWS
- PICK UP GARAGE
- PICK UP BASEMENT
- DUST/CLEAN BASEBOARDS
- GET RID OF ITEMS NO LONGER NEED
- ------------------------------
- ------------------------------
- ------------------------------

MON	KITCHEN	CLEAN KITCHEN TABLE
		WIPE DOWN SINK AND COUNTERS
		VACUUM OR MOP
		WIPE DOWN APPLIANCES

TUES	LIVINGROOM	PICK UP CLUTTER
		VACUUM OR MOP
		WASH BLANKETS
		DUST SURFACES

WED	BEDROOM	PUT AWAY CLOTHES/PICK UP CLUTTER
		DUST SURFACES
		WASH BEDDING
		VACUUM OR MOP

THUR	BATHROOM	SANITIZE TOILET
		VACUUM OR MOP
		WASH SHOWER,SINK AND MIRRORS
		WASH TOWELS AND MATS

FRI	DINING	CLEAN OFF TABLE
		VACUUM OR MOP
		DUST SURFACES
		PICK UP CLUTTER

SAT	ENTRY	SANTIZE DOORKNOBS
		DUST SURFACES
		VACUUM OR MOP
		PUT AWAY SHOES/COATS/HATS

SUN	GROCERY	CLEAN OUT FRIDGE
		MEAL PLAN
		GROCERY SHOP AND FILL GAS TANK
		MEAL PREP

DATE :

CLEANING CHEEKLIST

KEEP A GOOD THING GOING

EVERYDAY

	S	M	T	W	T	F	S
ONE LOAD OF LAUNDRY	◆	◆	◆	◆	◆	◆	◆
DISHES	◆	◆	◆	◆	◆	◆	◆
MAKE BEDS	◆	◆	◆	◆	◆	◆	◆
SPARY COUNTERTOPS	◆	◆	◆	◆	◆	◆	◆
PICK UP CLUTTER	◆	◆	◆	◆	◆	◆	◆
TRASH	◆	◆	◆	◆	◆	◆	◆
SORT MAIL	◆	◆	◆	◆	◆	◆	◆

MONTHLY

- ⬡ DUST CEILING FANS
- ⬡ CLEAN OVEN
- ⬡ CLEAN INSIDE OF FRIDGE
- ⬡ WASH WINDOWS
- ⬡ PICK UP GARAGE
- ⬡ PICK UP BASEMENT
- ⬡ DUST/CLEAN BASEBOARDS
- ⬡ GET RID OF ITEMS NO LONGER NEED
- ⬡ ----------------------------------
- ⬡ ----------------------------------
- ⬡ ----------------------------------
- ⬡ ----------------------------------

MON	KITCHEN	★ CLEAN KITCHEN TABLE ★ WIPE DOWN SINK AND COUNTERS ★ VACUUM OR MOP ★ WIPE DOWN APPLIANCES ★
TUES	LIVINGROOM	★ PICK UP CLUTTER ★ VACUUM OR MOP ★ WASH BLANKETS ★ DUST SURFACES ★
WED	BEDROOM	★ PUT AWAY CLOTHES/PICK UP CLUTTER ★ DUST SURFACES ★ WASH BEDDING ★ VACUUM OR MOP ★
THUR	BATHROOM	★ SANITIZE TOILET ★ VACUUM OR MOP ★ WASH SHOWER,SINK AND MIRRORS ★ WASH TOWELS AND MATS ★
FRI	DINING	★ CLEAN OFF TABLE ★ VACUUM OR MOP ★ DUST SURFACES ★ PICK UP CLUTTER ★
SAT	ENTRY	★ SANTIZE DOORKNOBS ★ DUST SURFACES ★ VACUUM OR MOP ★ PUT AWAY SHOES/COATS/HATS ★
SUN	GROCERY	★ CLEAN OUT FRIDGE ★ MEAL PLAN ★ GROCERY SHOP AND FILL GAS TANK ★ MEAL PREP ★

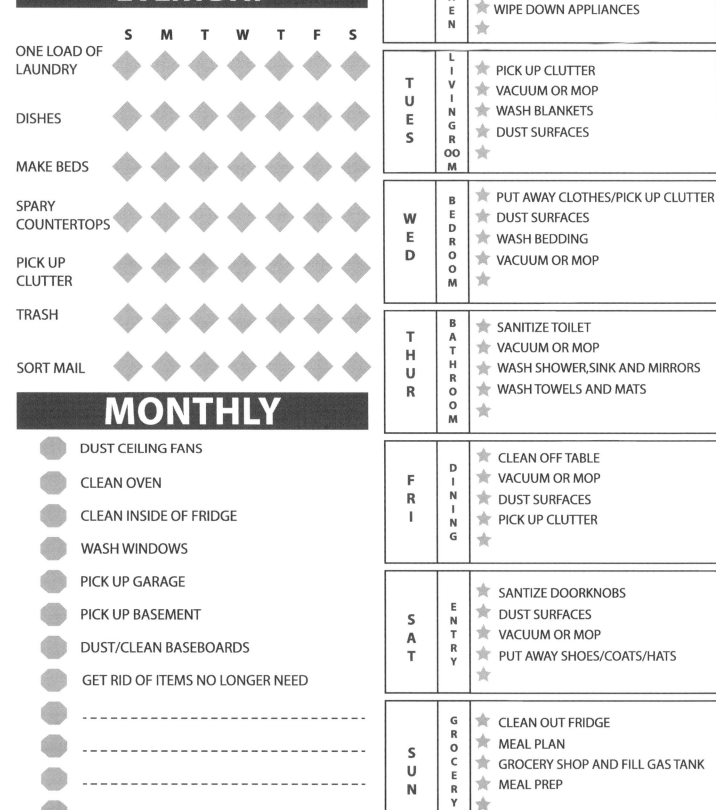

DATE :

CLEANING CHEEKLIST

KEEP A GOOD THING GOING

EVERYDAY

	S	M	T	W	T	F	S
ONE LOAD OF LAUNDRY	◆	◆	◆	◆	◆	◆	◆
DISHES	◆	◆	◆	◆	◆	◆	◆
MAKE BEDS	◆	◆	◆	◆	◆	◆	◆
SPARY COUNTERTOPS	◆	◆	◆	◆	◆	◆	◆
PICK UP CLUTTER	◆	◆	◆	◆	◆	◆	◆
TRASH	◆	◆	◆	◆	◆	◆	◆
SORT MAIL	◆	◆	◆	◆	◆	◆	◆

MONTHLY

- DUST CEILING FANS
- CLEAN OVEN
- CLEAN INSIDE OF FRIDGE
- WASH WINDOWS
- PICK UP GARAGE
- PICK UP BASEMENT
- DUST/CLEAN BASEBOARDS
- GET RID OF ITEMS NO LONGER NEED
- --------------------------
- --------------------------
- --------------------------

MON — KITCHEN
- ★ CLEAN KITCHEN TABLE
- ★ WIPE DOWN SINK AND COUNTERS
- ★ VACUUM OR MOP
- ★ WIPE DOWN APPLIANCES
- ★

TUES — LIVINGROOM
- ★ PICK UP CLUTTER
- ★ VACUUM OR MOP
- ★ WASH BLANKETS
- ★ DUST SURFACES
- ★

WED — BEDROOM
- ★ PUT AWAY CLOTHES/PICK UP CLUTTER
- ★ DUST SURFACES
- ★ WASH BEDDING
- ★ VACUUM OR MOP
- ★

THUR — BATHROOM
- ★ SANITIZE TOILET
- ★ VACUUM OR MOP
- ★ WASH SHOWER, SINK AND MIRRORS
- ★ WASH TOWELS AND MATS
- ★

FRI — DINING
- ★ CLEAN OFF TABLE
- ★ VACUUM OR MOP
- ★ DUST SURFACES
- ★ PICK UP CLUTTER
- ★

SAT — ENTRY
- ★ SANTIZE DOORKNOBS
- ★ DUST SURFACES
- ★ VACUUM OR MOP
- ★ PUT AWAY SHOES/COATS/HATS
- ★

SUN — GROCERY
- ★ CLEAN OUT FRIDGE
- ★ MEAL PLAN
- ★ GROCERY SHOP AND FILL GAS TANK
- ★ MEAL PREP

DATE :   # CLEANING CHEEKLIST

KEEP A GOOD THING GOING

EVERYDAY

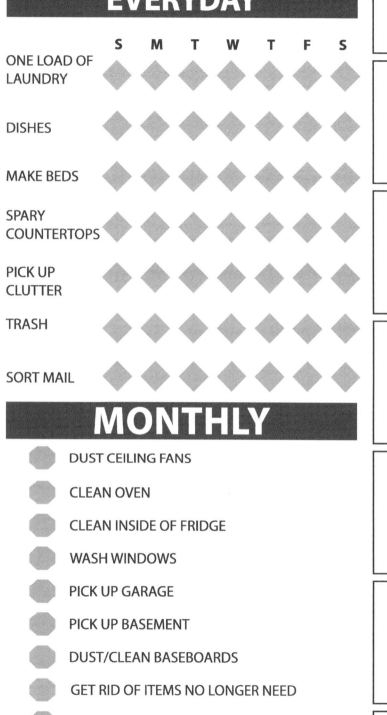

	S	M	T	W	T	F	S
ONE LOAD OF LAUNDRY	◆	◆	◆	◆	◆	◆	◆
DISHES	◆	◆	◆	◆	◆	◆	◆
MAKE BEDS	◆	◆	◆	◆	◆	◆	◆
SPARY COUNTERTOPS	◆	◆	◆	◆	◆	◆	◆
PICK UP CLUTTER	◆	◆	◆	◆	◆	◆	◆
TRASH	◆	◆	◆	◆	◆	◆	◆
SORT MAIL	◆	◆	◆	◆	◆	◆	◆

MONTHLY

- DUST CEILING FANS
- CLEAN OVEN
- CLEAN INSIDE OF FRIDGE
- WASH WINDOWS
- PICK UP GARAGE
- PICK UP BASEMENT
- DUST/CLEAN BASEBOARDS
- GET RID OF ITEMS NO LONGER NEED
- -
- -
- -
- -

MON — KITCHEN
- ★ CLEAN KITCHEN TABLE
- ★ WIPE DOWN SINK AND COUNTERS
- ★ VACUUM OR MOP
- ★ WIPE DOWN APPLIANCES
- ★

TUES — LIVINGROOM
- ★ PICK UP CLUTTER
- ★ VACUUM OR MOP
- ★ WASH BLANKETS
- ★ DUST SURFACES
- ★

WED — BEDROOM
- ★ PUT AWAY CLOTHES/PICK UP CLUTTER
- ★ DUST SURFACES
- ★ WASH BEDDING
- ★ VACUUM OR MOP
- ★

THUR — BATHROOM
- ★ SANITIZE TOILET
- ★ VACUUM OR MOP
- ★ WASH SHOWER,SINK AND MIRRORS
- ★ WASH TOWELS AND MATS
- ★

FRI — DINING
- ★ CLEAN OFF TABLE
- ★ VACUUM OR MOP
- ★ DUST SURFACES
- ★ PICK UP CLUTTER
- ★

SAT — ENTRY
- ★ SANTIZE DOORKNOBS
- ★ DUST SURFACES
- ★ VACUUM OR MOP
- ★ PUT AWAY SHOES/COATS/HATS
- ★

SUN — GROCERY
- ★ CLEAN OUT FRIDGE
- ★ MEAL PLAN
- ★ GROCERY SHOP AND FILL GAS TANK
- ★ MEAL PREP
- ★

DATE :

CLEANING CHEEKLIST

KEEP A GOOD THING GOING

EVERYDAY

	S	M	T	W	T	F	S
ONE LOAD OF LAUNDRY	◆	◆	◆	◆	◆	◆	◆
DISHES	◆	◆	◆	◆	◆	◆	◆
MAKE BEDS	◆	◆	◆	◆	◆	◆	◆
SPARY COUNTERTOPS	◆	◆	◆	◆	◆	◆	◆
PICK UP CLUTTER	◆	◆	◆	◆	◆	◆	◆
TRASH	◆	◆	◆	◆	◆	◆	◆
SORT MAIL	◆	◆	◆	◆	◆	◆	◆

MONTHLY

- ⬡ DUST CEILING FANS
- ⬡ CLEAN OVEN
- ⬡ CLEAN INSIDE OF FRIDGE
- ⬡ WASH WINDOWS
- ⬡ PICK UP GARAGE
- ⬡ PICK UP BASEMENT
- ⬡ DUST/CLEAN BASEBOARDS
- ⬡ GET RID OF ITEMS NO LONGER NEED
- ⬡ -
- ⬡ -
- ⬡ -
- ⬡ -

MON	KITCHEN	☆ CLEAN KITCHEN TABLE ☆ WIPE DOWN SINK AND COUNTERS ☆ VACUUM OR MOP ☆ WIPE DOWN APPLIANCES ☆
TUES	LIVING ROOM	☆ PICK UP CLUTTER ☆ VACUUM OR MOP ☆ WASH BLANKETS ☆ DUST SURFACES ☆
WED	BEDROOM	☆ PUT AWAY CLOTHES/PICK UP CLUTTER ☆ DUST SURFACES ☆ WASH BEDDING ☆ VACUUM OR MOP ☆
THUR	BATHROOM	☆ SANITIZE TOILET ☆ VACUUM OR MOP ☆ WASH SHOWER,SINK AND MIRRORS ☆ WASH TOWELS AND MATS ☆
FRI	DINING	☆ CLEAN OFF TABLE ☆ VACUUM OR MOP ☆ DUST SURFACES ☆ PICK UP CLUTTER ☆
SAT	ENTRY	☆ SANTIZE DOORKNOBS ☆ DUST SURFACES ☆ VACUUM OR MOP ☆ PUT AWAY SHOES/COATS/HATS ☆
SUN	GROCERY	☆ CLEAN OUT FRIDGE ☆ MEAL PLAN ☆ GROCERY SHOP AND FILL GAS TANK ☆ MEAL PREP

DATE :

CLEANING CHEEKLIST

KEEP A GOOD THING GOING

EVERYDAY

	S	M	T	W	T	F	S
ONE LOAD OF LAUNDRY	◆	◆	◆	◆	◆	◆	◆
DISHES	◆	◆	◆	◆	◆	◆	◆
MAKE BEDS	◆	◆	◆	◆	◆	◆	◆
SPARY COUNTERTOPS	◆	◆	◆	◆	◆	◆	◆
PICK UP CLUTTER	◆	◆	◆	◆	◆	◆	◆
TRASH	◆	◆	◆	◆	◆	◆	◆
SORT MAIL	◆	◆	◆	◆	◆	◆	◆

MONTHLY

- ⬡ DUST CEILING FANS
- ⬡ CLEAN OVEN
- ⬡ CLEAN INSIDE OF FRIDGE
- ⬡ WASH WINDOWS
- ⬡ PICK UP GARAGE
- ⬡ PICK UP BASEMENT
- ⬡ DUST/CLEAN BASEBOARDS
- ⬡ GET RID OF ITEMS NO LONGER NEED
- ⬡ -
- ⬡ -
- ⬡ -
- ⬡

MON	KITCHEN	★ CLEAN KITCHEN TABLE ★ WIPE DOWN SINK AND COUNTERS ★ VACUUM OR MOP ★ WIPE DOWN APPLIANCES ★
TUES	LIVING ROOM	★ PICK UP CLUTTER ★ VACUUM OR MOP ★ WASH BLANKETS ★ DUST SURFACES ★
WED	BEDROOM	★ PUT AWAY CLOTHES/PICK UP CLUTTER ★ DUST SURFACES ★ WASH BEDDING ★ VACUUM OR MOP ★
THUR	BATHROOM	★ SANITIZE TOILET ★ VACUUM OR MOP ★ WASH SHOWER, SINK AND MIRRORS ★ WASH TOWELS AND MATS ★
FRI	DINING	★ CLEAN OFF TABLE ★ VACUUM OR MOP ★ DUST SURFACES ★ PICK UP CLUTTER ★
SAT	ENTRY	★ SANTIZE DOORKNOBS ★ DUST SURFACES ★ VACUUM OR MOP ★ PUT AWAY SHOES/COATS/HATS ★
SUN	GROCERY	★ CLEAN OUT FRIDGE ★ MEAL PLAN ★ GROCERY SHOP AND FILL GAS TANK ★ MEAL PREP

DATE :

CLEANING CHEEKLIST

KEEP A GOOD THING GOING

EVERYDAY

	S	M	T	W	T	F	S
ONE LOAD OF LAUNDRY	◆	◆	◆	◆	◆	◆	◆
DISHES	◆	◆	◆	◆	◆	◆	◆
MAKE BEDS	◆	◆	◆	◆	◆	◆	◆
SPARY COUNTERTOPS	◆	◆	◆	◆	◆	◆	◆
PICK UP CLUTTER	◆	◆	◆	◆	◆	◆	◆
TRASH	◆	◆	◆	◆	◆	◆	◆
SORT MAIL	◆	◆	◆	◆	◆	◆	◆

MONTHLY

- DUST CEILING FANS
- CLEAN OVEN
- CLEAN INSIDE OF FRIDGE
- WASH WINDOWS
- PICK UP GARAGE
- PICK UP BASEMENT
- DUST/CLEAN BASEBOARDS
- GET RID OF ITEMS NO LONGER NEED
- -
- -
- -

MON	KITCHEN	★ CLEAN KITCHEN TABLE ★ WIPE DOWN SINK AND COUNTERS ★ VACUUM OR MOP ★ WIPE DOWN APPLIANCES ★
TUES	LIVING ROOM	★ PICK UP CLUTTER ★ VACUUM OR MOP ★ WASH BLANKETS ★ DUST SURFACES ★
WED	BEDROOM	★ PUT AWAY CLOTHES/PICK UP CLUTTER ★ DUST SURFACES ★ WASH BEDDING ★ VACUUM OR MOP ★
THUR	BATHROOM	★ SANITIZE TOILET ★ VACUUM OR MOP ★ WASH SHOWER,SINK AND MIRRORS ★ WASH TOWELS AND MATS ★
FRI	DINING	★ CLEAN OFF TABLE ★ VACUUM OR MOP ★ DUST SURFACES ★ PICK UP CLUTTER ★
SAT	ENTRY	★ SANTIZE DOORKNOBS ★ DUST SURFACES ★ VACUUM OR MOP ★ PUT AWAY SHOES/COATS/HATS ★
SUN	GROCERY	★ CLEAN OUT FRIDGE ★ MEAL PLAN ★ GROCERY SHOP AND FILL GAS TANK ★ MEAL PREP ★

DATE :

CLEANING CHEEKLIST

KEEP A GOOD THING GOING

EVERYDAY

	S	M	T	W	T	F	S
ONE LOAD OF LAUNDRY	◆	◆	◆	◆	◆	◆	◆
DISHES	◆	◆	◆	◆	◆	◆	◆
MAKE BEDS	◆	◆	◆	◆	◆	◆	◆
SPARY COUNTERTOPS	◆	◆	◆	◆	◆	◆	◆
PICK UP CLUTTER	◆	◆	◆	◆	◆	◆	◆
TRASH	◆	◆	◆	◆	◆	◆	◆
SORT MAIL	◆	◆	◆	◆	◆	◆	◆

MONTHLY

- DUST CEILING FANS
- CLEAN OVEN
- CLEAN INSIDE OF FRIDGE
- WASH WINDOWS
- PICK UP GARAGE
- PICK UP BASEMENT
- DUST/CLEAN BASEBOARDS
- GET RID OF ITEMS NO LONGER NEED
- _____
- _____
- _____
- _____

MON — **KITCHEN**
- ★ CLEAN KITCHEN TABLE
- ★ WIPE DOWN SINK AND COUNTERS
- ★ VACUUM OR MOP
- ★ WIPE DOWN APPLIANCES
- ★

TUES — **LIVINGROOM**
- ★ PICK UP CLUTTER
- ★ VACUUM OR MOP
- ★ WASH BLANKETS
- ★ DUST SURFACES
- ★

WED — **BEDROOM**
- ★ PUT AWAY CLOTHES/PICK UP CLUTTER
- ★ DUST SURFACES
- ★ WASH BEDDING
- ★ VACUUM OR MOP
- ★

THUR — **BATHROOM**
- ★ SANITIZE TOILET
- ★ VACUUM OR MOP
- ★ WASH SHOWER,SINK AND MIRRORS
- ★ WASH TOWELS AND MATS
- ★

FRI — **DINING**
- ★ CLEAN OFF TABLE
- ★ VACUUM OR MOP
- ★ DUST SURFACES
- ★ PICK UP CLUTTER
- ★

SAT — **ENTRY**
- ★ SANTIZE DOORKNOBS
- ★ DUST SURFACES
- ★ VACUUM OR MOP
- ★ PUT AWAY SHOES/COATS/HATS
- ★

SUN — **GROCERY**
- ★ CLEAN OUT FRIDGE
- ★ MEAL PLAN
- ★ GROCERY SHOP AND FILL GAS TANK
- ★ MEAL PREP

DATE :

CLEANING CHEEKLIST

KEEP A GOOD THING GOING

EVERYDAY

	S	M	T	W	T	F	S
ONE LOAD OF LAUNDRY	◆	◆	◆	◆	◆	◆	◆
DISHES	◆	◆	◆	◆	◆	◆	◆
MAKE BEDS	◆	◆	◆	◆	◆	◆	◆
SPARY COUNTERTOPS	◆	◆	◆	◆	◆	◆	◆
PICK UP CLUTTER	◆	◆	◆	◆	◆	◆	◆
TRASH	◆	◆	◆	◆	◆	◆	◆
SORT MAIL	◆	◆	◆	◆	◆	◆	◆

MONTHLY

- DUST CEILING FANS
- CLEAN OVEN
- CLEAN INSIDE OF FRIDGE
- WASH WINDOWS
- PICK UP GARAGE
- PICK UP BASEMENT
- DUST/CLEAN BASEBOARDS
- GET RID OF ITEMS NO LONGER NEED
- ------------------------------
- ------------------------------
- ------------------------------

MON — KITCHEN
- ★ CLEAN KITCHEN TABLE
- ★ WIPE DOWN SINK AND COUNTERS
- ★ VACUUM OR MOP
- ★ WIPE DOWN APPLIANCES
- ★

TUES — LIVINGROOM
- ★ PICK UP CLUTTER
- ★ VACUUM OR MOP
- ★ WASH BLANKETS
- ★ DUST SURFACES
- ★

WED — BEDROOM
- ★ PUT AWAY CLOTHES/PICK UP CLUTTER
- ★ DUST SURFACES
- ★ WASH BEDDING
- ★ VACUUM OR MOP
- ★

THUR — BATHROOM
- ★ SANITIZE TOILET
- ★ VACUUM OR MOP
- ★ WASH SHOWER, SINK AND MIRRORS
- ★ WASH TOWELS AND MATS
- ★

FRI — DINING
- ★ CLEAN OFF TABLE
- ★ VACUUM OR MOP
- ★ DUST SURFACES
- ★ PICK UP CLUTTER

SAT — ENTRY
- ★ SANTIZE DOORKNOBS
- ★ DUST SURFACES
- ★ VACUUM OR MOP
- ★ PUT AWAY SHOES/COATS/HATS

SUN — GROCERY
- ★ CLEAN OUT FRIDGE
- ★ MEAL PLAN
- ★ GROCERY SHOP AND FILL GAS TANK
- ★ MEAL PREP

DATE :

CLEANING CHEEKLIST

KEEP A GOOD THING GOING

EVERYDAY

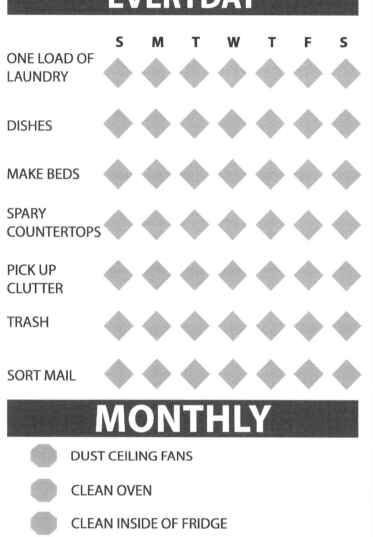

	S	M	T	W	T	F	S
ONE LOAD OF LAUNDRY	◆	◆	◆	◆	◆	◆	◆
DISHES	◆	◆	◆	◆	◆	◆	◆
MAKE BEDS	◆	◆	◆	◆	◆	◆	◆
SPARY COUNTERTOPS	◆	◆	◆	◆	◆	◆	◆
PICK UP CLUTTER	◆	◆	◆	◆	◆	◆	◆
TRASH	◆	◆	◆	◆	◆	◆	◆
SORT MAIL	◆	◆	◆	◆	◆	◆	◆

MONTHLY

- ⬡ DUST CEILING FANS
- ⬡ CLEAN OVEN
- ⬡ CLEAN INSIDE OF FRIDGE
- ⬡ WASH WINDOWS
- ⬡ PICK UP GARAGE
- ⬡ PICK UP BASEMENT
- ⬡ DUST/CLEAN BASEBOARDS
- ⬡ GET RID OF ITEMS NO LONGER NEED
- ⬡ -------------------------------
- ⬡ -------------------------------
- ⬡ -------------------------------
- ⬡

MON — KITCHEN
- ★ CLEAN KITCHEN TABLE
- ★ WIPE DOWN SINK AND COUNTERS
- ★ VACUUM OR MOP
- ★ WIPE DOWN APPLIANCES
- ★

TUES — LIVINGROOM
- ★ PICK UP CLUTTER
- ★ VACUUM OR MOP
- ★ WASH BLANKETS
- ★ DUST SURFACES
- ★

WED — BEDROOM
- ★ PUT AWAY CLOTHES/PICK UP CLUTTER
- ★ DUST SURFACES
- ★ WASH BEDDING
- ★ VACUUM OR MOP
- ★

THUR — BATHROOM
- ★ SANITIZE TOILET
- ★ VACUUM OR MOP
- ★ WASH SHOWER,SINK AND MIRRORS
- ★ WASH TOWELS AND MATS
- ★

FRI — DINING
- ★ CLEAN OFF TABLE
- ★ VACUUM OR MOP
- ★ DUST SURFACES
- ★ PICK UP CLUTTER
- ★

SAT — ENTRY
- ★ SANTIZE DOORKNOBS
- ★ DUST SURFACES
- ★ VACUUM OR MOP
- ★ PUT AWAY SHOES/COATS/HATS
- ★

SUN — GROCERY
- ★ CLEAN OUT FRIDGE
- ★ MEAL PLAN
- ★ GROCERY SHOP AND FILL GAS TANK
- ★ MEAL PREP
- ★

DATE :

CLEANING CHEEKLIST

KEEP A GOOD THING GOING

EVERYDAY

	S	M	T	W	T	F	S
ONE LOAD OF LAUNDRY	◆	◆	◆	◆	◆	◆	◆
DISHES	◆	◆	◆	◆	◆	◆	◆
MAKE BEDS	◆	◆	◆	◆	◆	◆	◆
SPARY COUNTERTOPS	◆	◆	◆	◆	◆	◆	◆
PICK UP CLUTTER	◆	◆	◆	◆	◆	◆	◆
TRASH	◆	◆	◆	◆	◆	◆	◆
SORT MAIL	◆	◆	◆	◆	◆	◆	◆

MONTHLY

- DUST CEILING FANS
- CLEAN OVEN
- CLEAN INSIDE OF FRIDGE
- WASH WINDOWS
- PICK UP GARAGE
- PICK UP BASEMENT
- DUST/CLEAN BASEBOARDS
- GET RID OF ITEMS NO LONGER NEED
- -
- -
- -

MON — KITCHEN
- ★ CLEAN KITCHEN TABLE
- ★ WIPE DOWN SINK AND COUNTERS
- ★ VACUUM OR MOP
- ★ WIPE DOWN APPLIANCES
- ★

TUES — LIVING ROOM
- ★ PICK UP CLUTTER
- ★ VACUUM OR MOP
- ★ WASH BLANKETS
- ★ DUST SURFACES
- ★

WED — BEDROOM
- ★ PUT AWAY CLOTHES/PICK UP CLUTTER
- ★ DUST SURFACES
- ★ WASH BEDDING
- ★ VACUUM OR MOP
- ★

THUR — BATHROOM
- ★ SANITIZE TOILET
- ★ VACUUM OR MOP
- ★ WASH SHOWER,SINK AND MIRRORS
- ★ WASH TOWELS AND MATS
- ★

FRI — DINING
- ★ CLEAN OFF TABLE
- ★ VACUUM OR MOP
- ★ DUST SURFACES
- ★ PICK UP CLUTTER
- ★

SAT — ENTRY
- ★ SANTIZE DOORKNOBS
- ★ DUST SURFACES
- ★ VACUUM OR MOP
- ★ PUT AWAY SHOES/COATS/HATS
- ★

SUN — GROCERY
- ★ CLEAN OUT FRIDGE
- ★ MEAL PLAN
- ★ GROCERY SHOP AND FILL GAS TANK
- ★ MEAL PREP
- ★

DATE :　CLEANING CHEEKLIST

KEEP A GOOD THING GOING

EVERYDAY

	S	M	T	W	T	F	S
ONE LOAD OF LAUNDRY	◆	◆	◆	◆	◆	◆	◆
DISHES	◆	◆	◆	◆	◆	◆	◆
MAKE BEDS	◆	◆	◆	◆	◆	◆	◆
SPARY COUNTERTOPS	◆	◆	◆	◆	◆	◆	◆
PICK UP CLUTTER	◆	◆	◆	◆	◆	◆	◆
TRASH	◆	◆	◆	◆	◆	◆	◆
SORT MAIL	◆	◆	◆	◆	◆	◆	◆

MONTHLY

- DUST CEILING FANS
- CLEAN OVEN
- CLEAN INSIDE OF FRIDGE
- WASH WINDOWS
- PICK UP GARAGE
- PICK UP BASEMENT
- DUST/CLEAN BASEBOARDS
- GET RID OF ITEMS NO LONGER NEED
- _____
- _____
- _____

MON — KITCHEN
- ★ CLEAN KITCHEN TABLE
- ★ WIPE DOWN SINK AND COUNTERS
- ★ VACUUM OR MOP
- ★ WIPE DOWN APPLIANCES
- ★

TUES — LIVINGROOM
- ★ PICK UP CLUTTER
- ★ VACUUM OR MOP
- ★ WASH BLANKETS
- ★ DUST SURFACES
- ★

WED — BEDROOM
- ★ PUT AWAY CLOTHES/PICK UP CLUTTER
- ★ DUST SURFACES
- ★ WASH BEDDING
- ★ VACUUM OR MOP
- ★

THUR — BATHROOM
- ★ SANITIZE TOILET
- ★ VACUUM OR MOP
- ★ WASH SHOWER,SINK AND MIRRORS
- ★ WASH TOWELS AND MATS
- ★

FRI — DINING
- ★ CLEAN OFF TABLE
- ★ VACUUM OR MOP
- ★ DUST SURFACES
- ★ PICK UP CLUTTER
- ★

SAT — ENTRY
- ★ SANTIZE DOORKNOBS
- ★ DUST SURFACES
- ★ VACUUM OR MOP
- ★ PUT AWAY SHOES/COATS/HATS
- ★

SUN — GROCERY
- ★ CLEAN OUT FRIDGE
- ★ MEAL PLAN
- ★ GROCERY SHOP AND FILL GAS TANK
- ★ MEAL PREP
- ★

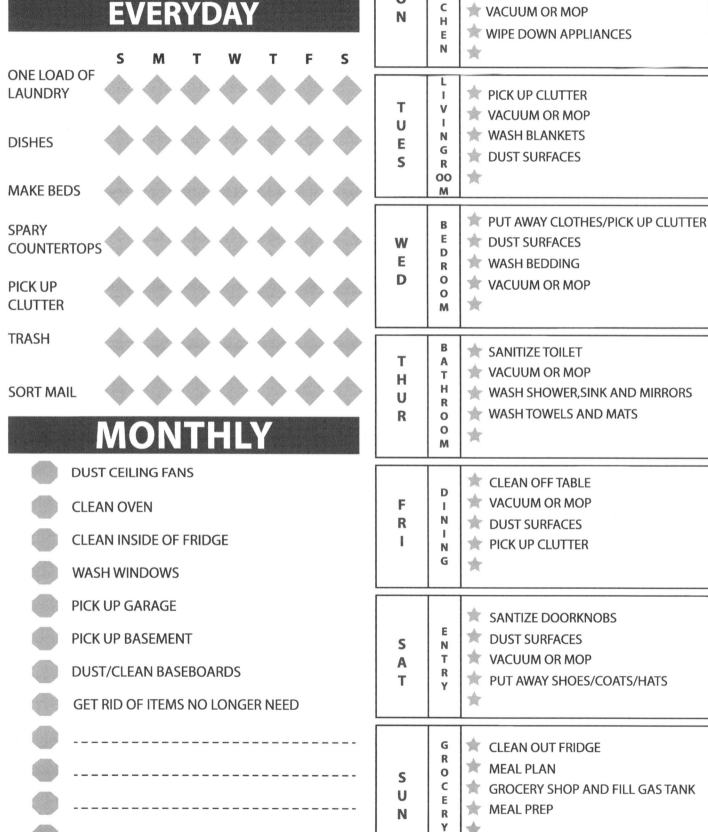

Made in the USA
Las Vegas, NV
21 March 2022

46089089R00061